W9-BYS-989

HOW TO
DODGE
A
DRAGON

A DEVOTIONAL
READING
OF REVELATION

Mark E. Moore

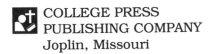

COLLEGE PRESS
PUBLISHING COMPANY
Joplin, Missouri

International Standard Book Number 0-89900-828-3

CONTENTS

To Barbara,
Like this Revelation you are a mystery
far too deep and wonderful for me to understand.
Like this book you comfort my soul
and usher my spirit to the boundaries of heaven.
And like this vision, the darker my days,
the more I cling to the beauty of your presence.

STUDIES FOR SMALL GROUPS

Welcome to the *Studies for Small Groups* series from College Press. This series is designed for simplicity of use while giving insight into important issues of the Christian life. Some, like the present volume, are scriptural studies. Others are more topical in nature.

A number of possible uses could be made of this study. Because there are a limited number of lessons, the format is ideal for new or potential Christians who can begin the study without feeling that they are tied into an overly long commitment. It could also be used for one or two months of weekly studies by a home Bible study group. The series is suitable for individual as well as group study.

Of course, any study is only as good as the effort you put into it. The group leader should study each lesson carefully before the group study session, and if possible, come up with additional Scriptures and other supporting material. Although study questions are provided for each lesson, it would also be helpful if the leader can add his or her own questions.

Neither is it necessary to complete a full lesson in one class period. If the discussion is going well, don't feel that you have to cut it off to fit time constraints, as long as the discussion is related to the topic and not off on side issues.

Because there is now more interest in prophecy than at almost any other time in world history, but much confusion as well, College Press is happy to present this new nine-lesson study in the *Studies for Small Groups* series, *How to Dodge a Dragon*.

One caution is in order. Neither the author nor the publishers intend this study to be a definitive interpretation of the precise meaning of various prophecies in the book of Revelation. Rather it is what its subtitle indicates — a *devotional* reading that teaches us the broad lessons of the book. Some interpretation of the visions is inevitable and you may not agree 100% with those interpretations, but this should not distract from the overall thematic development of this study guide. The intent of the author is more clearly stated in the following introduction to the study.

HOW TO DODGE
A DRAGON

The book you now hold in your hand is not a commentary in the usual sense. It is not designed to tell you what each verse means. Rather, it is designed to ask, "How should this message change the way I live my life?" In other words, commentaries address the head. This book will address the heart and the hands.

The most important question to ask of this book is not, "When will Jesus return?" or even "How will the world come to an end?" Rather, the crucial question is, "How should Christians live in a world so warped as ours?" Eschatology (that is, "end-times" talk), in the Bible is surprisingly practical. Whether you are talking about Matthew 24, 1 Thessalonians 4, or even 2 Peter 3, the advice is always the same — Be Ready!

What, pray tell, is the biblical advice for preparing for Jesus' return? Should we buy a bomb shelter and stock it with food? Should we congregate on a desert mountaintop? Should we I.D. the Antichrist and preach against the league of ten nations? No, the Bible simply tells us to live holy and godly lives. It tells us to cling to Jesus for dear life. It adjures us to fix our eyes on Jesus, to clean up the church, to worship vigorously, and above all, to stand firm in our faith until the end.

Revelation is often approached as a calendar. Some look at it as a history book that describes the Decian persecution of the first century. Others believe it tells primarily of yet future events. Both try to pin each symbol to a date on a calendar. That creates a problem, however. If this book is primarily about the past, then it is not very motivating for us today. If it is primarily about the present, then it was largely irrelevant to John's original audience. Either way, most Christians throughout the history of the church who have applied Revelation to themselves have been mostly wrong.

But what if Revelation is not viewed as a calendar but as a template? What if we are able to lay its principles over any period of suffering? Then most Christians throughout the history of the church who have applied Revelation to themselves have been mostly right. That is not to say that John did not have a historic reality in mind when he wrote the book. It is to say, however, that like the prophecies of the Old Testament, there are principles and metaphors imbedded in them that are contemporary and relevant for each generation. That's why this book has perpetual relevance. Wherever there is tragedy or suffering, persecuted Christians or rampant evil, this book weaves its way into the life of the church, reminding God's people of their security in Christ, the seriousness of their spiritual warfare, and the wondrous sovereignty of our mighty God.

In the opening chapter, Jesus promises a blessing for those who read and obey this book (1:3). Therefore, any believer who reads this book and walks away scared rather than strengthened has misread it. Here's the bottom line. This book is not Nostradamus' diary of end-times events as much as it is a pilgrim's guide through times of suffering. It won't answer all your questions, but it will shine a light at the end of a dark tunnel to guide you through your tribulation. As such, I suspect that those who suffer most will understand best this marvelous book called Revelation. To those Christians facing physical persecution, this book makes sense. To those believers ravaged by seemingly senseless suffering, this book brings healing. To those saints who are at the end of their rope, this book brings hope. To this end I pray that the following pages will magnify the light this book sheds on your own personal pilgrimage.

1

THREE PORTRAITS OF JESUS

Revelation is a pretty slippery book when you try to grab hold of it. What exactly does it mean? For starters, we might assume that the book of Revelation reveals things. That is, it uncovers stuff. After all, isn't that what the title claims? This is no new "revelation" about Revelation. Martin Luther came to the same conclusion. In fact, he said the book of Revelation ought to be kicked out of the Bible because it doesn't reveal much of anything. Luther may seem extreme, but he is hard to argue with. After all, most people who read through Revelation walk away more confused than when they came. If it's supposed to uncover stuff, it doesn't seem to be working.

Part of the problem is that we typically spend most of our time on individual symbols like 666 or stinging grasshoppers. As a result, we miss the broad principles of the book. In other words, we count brush strokes instead of looking at the big picture. So, if we stopped concentrating on individual symbols, and looked at the broad brush strokes, we might just see what God is trying to tell us. As a matter of fact, the book of Revelation *does* uncover stuff, important stuff! Stuff like eternity. Here we have a blueprint for heaven. Stuff like Jesus' return and how he's going to right all wrongs. That's important stuff. It helps us deal with this question, "Why do bad things happen to good people?" That's *huge!* We are all aware that we are in a spiritual battle between evil and good. As the curtain rises in Revelation, behind the physical veil we get a glimpse of the spiritual realities with which we deal daily. All of this is important stuff. And that's what this book reveals. Yet of all its revelations the most magnificent is this: The person of Jesus.

Undoubtedly you already know what Jesus looks like. You've seen his picture in the foyer at church. The problem is that Jesus is not Scandinavian. He is Jewish. Hence, you probably need to darken his skin just a bit. And let's make those eyes brown or black. Furthermore, if you have a morphing program on your computer you might want to do something about that Roman nose. He is, after all, Jewish.

Let's say, for the sake of argument, that you do picture Jesus as a first century Palestinian. Even so, that is a thin slice of his existence. For only thirty-three years did Jesus put on skin. Long before that he had an eternal history. And since that time his portrait looks very different from the one in the halls of your home. *The book of Revelation tells us what Jesus really looks like. It draws three pictures for us.* Take a look.

JESUS THE GREAT HIGH PRIEST

In the very first chapter John is sitting on a rock in the middle of the Aegean Sea, stranded in exile. It is the Lord's day, so he is worshiping, praying, minding his own business. Somewhere in the middle of the third verse of "How Great Thou Art" Jesus sneaks up behind him and scares the wits out of him. In verse 11 Jesus shouts at John from behind: "Write on a scroll what you see and send it to the seven churches." John turns around and there is this colossal high priest. How do we know he is a high priest? He is dressed like one. His robe reaches down to his feet and his sash is solid gold. There he is, standing among lampstands. That is just like a high priest. He is awesome from his sideburns to his sandals. His feet look

The book of Revelation tells us what Jesus really looks like. It draws three pictures for us.

10

like bronze fresh from a flaming furnace. We have here a high priest that leaves charcoal in his wake as he walks across Patmos. His hair is white like wool. To American eyes he looks like an old man, but if you put on Jewish goggles, you begin to see God. Surely John was thinking about Daniel 7:9 when he writes those words. Daniel

John sees the divine and the human blended together right down where he lives.

says, "As I looked, thrones were set in place, and the Ancient of Days took his seat." Why, that's God himself! Daniel describes him: His clothing was "white as snow; the hair of his head was white like wool." Flash back to Revelation. Through John's eyes you expect to see Jesus. Instead you see God in the garb of a high priest. Father and Son are now one and the same.

Jesus is also described as a "Son of Man." That sounds familiar. It comes straight out of the Gospels. Jesus alone referred to himself as "Son of Man." You think he is bragging? Hardly. In the Old Testament the phrase "son of man" is used 100 times and 93 of those are in Ezekiel. Every time God calls Ezekiel "son of man" he is not lifting him up but putting him in his place. He is saying "I am God. You're 'son of man.' You are human — warts, pimples and all. A human-human." There is only one verse in the O.T. that doesn't fit that pattern. It is in Daniel 7:14. We've been there before. Remember? This is the vision of the Ancient of Days. Toward the tail end of the vision it says, "There before me was one like a son of man, coming with the clouds of heaven." That's very odd because when you hear "son of man" you think "human," but when you hear "clouds of heaven" you think "God." Suddenly the two have commingled up where God dwells. That is the Old Testament. In the New Testament the two have commingled down where men dwell. Suddenly when John turns around, what he expects to see is Jesus, but what he sees is God. *He sees the divine and the human blended together right down where he lives.* That is picture number one.

11

JESUS THE LAMB OF GOD

Picture number two comes from chapter five of the book of Revelation. John sneaks into the throne room of God and gets a glimpse of the Almighty. In his right hand God holds a scroll, written on both sides. John is as curious as a cat. He wants to know what is in the scroll. But in all the glories of heaven, all the magistrates hanging around, the elders, the beasts, the creatures, the angels, not one of them is worthy to open the scroll! John starts to cry. He cries and cries because no one is worthy to open the scroll. Then an angel comes up to comfort him and says "Don't cry anymore because there is one, just one, but there is one, who is worthy to open the scroll. He is the lion of the tribe of Judah." The drum roll begins. From stage left out walks . . . you think the lion of the tribe of Judah. Yet as if some demented stage hand has played a cruel joke, he sends out this lamb that has been slain. What's going on here? He said that he was the lion of the tribe of Judah and out walks this pathetic looking lamb. Don't misunderstand. The lamb, though slain, is now very much alive. And although this lamb has been badly beaten, he is no weakling. It still seems silly, however, to compare a slaughtered sheep with a victorious lion. Doesn't it?

What do you do with a lamb like that? When you see him, there is only one thing that you can do — worship him. Watch as *all of heaven comes to its feet in chapter five to worship the lamb.*

"Then I looked and heard the voice of many angels, numbering thousands upon thousands, and ten thousand times ten thousand. They encircled the throne and the living creatures and the elders. In a loud voice they sang:
'Worthy is the Lamb, who was slain,
to receive power and wealth and
wisdom and strength
and honor and glory and praise!'"

That is picture number two.

All of heaven comes to its feet to worship the lamb.

A KING ARRAYED FOR BATTLE

Picture number three comes from chapter nineteen of the book of Revelation.

It opens up with the hallelujah chorus. Verse one: "'Hallelujah! Salvation and glory and power belong to our God.'" Skip down to verse three: "And again they shouted: 'Hallelujah! The smoke from her goes up for ever and ever.'" Again in verse four: "'Amen, Hallelujah!' Then a voice came from the throne saying: 'Praise our God, all you his servants, you who fear him, both small and great.'" One last time in verse six, after peals of thunder and shouting: "'Hallelujah! For our Lord God Almighty reigns. Let us rejoice and be glad and give him glory! For the wedding of the Lamb has come, and his bride has made herself ready.'" These are the only four uses of the word "hallelujah" in the New Testament. It's exciting!

When heaven's gates are kicked open, it is not a bridegroom who comes out but a conquering king.

We are getting ready for a wedding. There is going to be a feast for the bridegroom. So you expect that out from stage right will come a groom. Yet *when heaven's gates are kicked open, it is not a bridegroom who comes out but a conquering king.* He rides on a white stallion with many crowns on his head. We recognize those eyes of fire and his sharp tongue from chapter one. He is unmistakably the Christ of God. When he appeared in Matthew he wore a Galilean's garb. When he returns in Revelation, he dons a robe dipped in blood. When he first came he held a shepherd's staff, next time it will be an iron scepter. And notice: he has no shield because he doesn't need one. Last time he wore a crown of thorns. On his return, he will bear many crowns of victory. In the incarnation his name was "Son of Man." At his inauguration His name is tattooed to his thigh "KING OF KINGS AND LORD OF LORDS." He is unparalleled in power. Satan and all his henchmen on earth, the kings and rulers of evil, cower before him. You expect at the beginning of this chapter to have a bridegroom's banquet, but at the end of the chapter you get a buzzard's buffet: "The rest of them were killed with the sword that came out of the mouth of the rider on the horse, and all the birds gorged themselves on their flesh" (19:21). It is grotesque and wonderful all at once. That is picture number three.

So what? It is entertaining stuff, but what does that have to do with today? Perhaps you didn't notice, but each of these pictures precedes one of the greatest struggles the church faces. This great high priest of chapter 1 stands before the seven churches of chapters 2-3. Be honest. Have you never been frustrated with the church? Indeed she is Christ's bride, but at times it seems like the Master should get a divorce. Admit it, the church is often filled with little people complaining about stupid things. We spin our wheels in ignorant theological debates. We fill the local news with sexual scandal and financial mismanagement. Sometimes the church is an embarrassment. We say we want to be the New Testament Church. Congratulations, we made it! The descriptions in chapters two and three are just like churches today, and it's not a pretty picture! Isn't God going to do anything? Answer: Yes! Sometimes we get to feeling like God has taken a vacation. Perhaps he is not paying attention even to what the church is doing.

Take another look at the high priest of chapter one. You will notice that he is standing amidst seven lampstands. In 1:20, John gives us an inspired interpretation of these lampstands: "The mystery of the seven stars that you saw on my right hand and of the seven gold lampstands is this: The seven stars are the angels of the seven churches, and the seven lampstands are the seven churches." So what does it mean? Jesus stands amidst these churches that are as messed up as any you've ever attended. You may not see him with your eyes, but if you'll allow John, he will give you the vision to see Christ today. He is here. He is now. If you think he is far away, not paying much attention to what you are doing or how you are living, you are badly mistaken. *God is here and he will respond to the sin of his church and that ought to change the way we live our lives.* If you think that God is on vacation, you had better take another look at the high priest. Look again. Look again to the High Priest of God.

God will respond to the sin of his church and that ought to change the way we live our lives.

A second struggle we face is the suffering of good people. In chapter six of this book, when Jesus opens the scroll,

14

out march four horses. One is black, one is white, one is red, and one is pale. They represent death and war, bloodshed and famine. All around the world today are Christian brothers and sisters that are in the throes of war. In the Middle East, South Africa, China, and South America our Christian brothers are experiencing these four horrible horsemen breathing down their necks.

Who has not asked the question: "Why do bad things happen to good people?"

It would probably be inappropriate for us who are couched in the comforts of America, to compare our suffering to the kind of suffering Christians experience around the world. Still, *who has not asked the question: "Why do bad things happen to good people?"* Why do young men die in the prime of life leaving thirty year old widows and children without fathers? Why do godly women miscarry? Why do ministers lose their homes in natural disasters? Why do little children have pot bellies? Why do women get beat up in their own homes right here in our neighborhoods? Surely God can do something. Surely he should!

About the time we get angry and want to shout at God we remember that there is a lamb in chapter five. We need to take another look at this lamb. One of the things we notice is that his scars are greater than ours. When we point the finger at Jesus and say "You just don't understand! I'm lonely." He shouts back, "I do understand!" When we say to God, "But my friend abandoned me," the Lamb replies, "I understand!" When we say to God, "My body hurts," he says "I know, mine does too!" Everything we say to Christ he says back to us "I understand." That doesn't take the pain away but at least we don't have to go through it alone. All of us experience suffering at some level at some time in our lives. Suffering is neither unnatural nor unbearable. What is unbearable is suffering alone. There is good news in this Revelation: Christians don't ever have to suffer alone. The Lamb of God stands at our side bloodied and sympathetic. When we weep, he shares our tears. When we sigh, his Spirit intercedes. When we are weak and battered, his

15

strength bolsters us. It is good news indeed that this lamb is a victorious lion.

There is something else about this lamb. He has scars all over him . . . and they're all mine. Not only is his suffering greater than mine, his suffering IS mine. I'm redeemed by the blood of the Lamb. That changes everything! He died in my stead so that I might live in his likeness. As a result, you can destroy my body, you can burn my belongings, you can blaspheme my name, but you will never touch my soul. The blood of the Lamb secures my position with God. His purchase means I'm possessed by the Holy One. Now, that doesn't remove the pain of temporal travail, but it does secure my salvation, and that is comforting in the extreme. All other earthly pursuits, pleasures and priorities pale against the backdrop of our eternal salvation. You've just got to look at the lamb. *When you think that God doesn't understand, you take a look at the lamb.*

A third struggle for the Christian is our uncertain future. The most difficult chapter of this book is chapter 20. We have the thousand years, Satan being bound, a lake of fire. When? How? Who? The fact of the matter is we just don't know! A lot of very smart people take educated guesses, but that's about the best we have to offer. The bottom line is that we do not know what the future holds. We worry about what the world is going to be like when our kids grow up. What are they going to have to put up with and live in? Racial prejudice is running rampant. Violence and pornography continue to rise, often as partners. We feel the weight of governmental corruption and gangs in our neighborhoods. When is it all going to end? Is there no jumping off place for a world gone awry? What do you do when it seems like God is never going to stop what is going on?

When you think that God doesn't understand, you take a look at the lamb.

You need to take another look at chapter nineteen. There we find a king mounting a horse, perhaps as we speak. He is coming back. That's a promise! He will right these wrongs. For all that Satan has done, there will

16

be hell to pay, not only for him and his demons, but for all who participate with him. The kings of this earth, the governors, the rulers, the rich and the mighty, the corrupt and the lowly — all those with the mark of the beast — will be thrown into the lake of fire. I don't

For all of our major troubles in life, this book has the answer.

know why God is waiting, I wish he would come today. But as surely as he has kept every other promise he ever made, you can bet he'll keep this one! I know he is coming, and with him, retribution. While that doesn't remove my pain, it does make it palatable for the time being. When you think that God is unresponsive, you look again at chapter nineteen. You look again at the coming King.

For all of our major troubles in life, this book has the answer. Take a look. Take a look at a high priest, a lamb, and a soon coming king. For by fixing our eyes on Jesus, we see more clearly how to live through the complexities of life.

REFLECTING ON LESSON ONE

1. List the kinds of things Revelation reveals. Circle two things on this list you personally will look for in this study.

2. What things in this portrait surprise you, comfort you, and unsettle you?

3. Discuss what might happen if Jesus appeared in the midst of your study group right now. How would it change you and your practical daily living? Could this text function in the same way for you as a physical appearance of Jesus?

4. What changes would take place in your church if Jesus was seen with its lampstand? How can you, in a constructive way, make Jesus more visible in your church to promote these changes?

5. Share with the study group your personal suffering in life. Discuss together how a view of the slain-victorious Lamb comforts Christians in times of trouble.

6. How would a clear view of our soon coming king alter your personal behavior today? Have each person share at least one practical change they would make.

7. As a group, out loud, memorize Hebrews 12:2.

2
T W O

GOD'S TRACK RECORD WITH WOMEN

God has a pretty poor track record with women. I am not talking about disciples, but about his fiancées. In the Old Testament he was betrothed to a prostitute. At least that is what he told the prophets (Jer. 2; Ezek. 16, 23; Hosea 2). He accused Israel of adultery via idolatry. He made his point poignantly when he asked Hosea to go to the red light district of Jerusalem and find himself a woman. "Marry her," he said. For most preachers, if God told them to marry a prostitute, that would surely count as a bad day.

Then comes the New Testament. We find that the Bride of Christ, in all her glory, is, well, an adulteress. That is what James says in chapter four verse four: "You adulterous people, don't you know that friendship with the world is hatred towards God?" The Lord has just had a rough time with women. So it is no surprise that he has a lot to say to his Bride in Revelation (2-3).

It's kind of dangerous to bad-mouth another man's bride. One ought not to walk into a wedding and bellow: "Hey, who's the chunk in the white dress?" That's a fast lane to pain. Therefore, far be it from me to dare to say anything about the Bride of Christ that he has not already said. Nonetheless, he said a mouthful in these two chapters.

You've heard this story before. If you've read Shakespeare you recognize here *The Taming of the Shrew*. What a play! That is Revelation two and three. For those with a little less culture, we could talk about *My Fair Lady*. It's the same plot. For those completely devoid of culture, we might revert to Hollywood's rendition of *Pretty Woman*. They're all the same. You've got a guy who is pretty rich or pretty smart. He finds this woman with serious flaws to her disposition, her education, or her occupation. Nevertheless, the hero comes along and sees something in her that captivates him. So he woos her. He loves her. And his love transforms her into a beautiful woman fit for a king.

That is the biography of the church. God adores you. *When nobody else sees what he sees, when nobody else loves what he loves, he is at work transforming you into a bride that is fit for a king.* Granted, his bride presently needs a face lift. That's precisely what these two chapters are all about.

What we have here are seven letters. Actually there is only one letter — a form letter. It is reproduced seven times with a few minor changes to make it fit each individual congregation. There are three parts to this form letter. Part "A" is the characteristic of Christ that is taken from the vision of the great high priest in chapter one. Each letter highlights one of the aspects of Christ as if to say, the one who is giving you a spanking right now has the authority to do so. He is not a peasant Palestinian; he is the Living Lord, the Great High Priest.

Part "B" is an evaluation of the church. These descriptions are surprisingly contemporary. We had better listen carefully as we eavesdrop on somebody else's mail.

> When nobody else sees what he sees or loves what he loves, he is at work transforming you into a bride that is fit for a king.

Part "C" of this form letter, in a variety of ways, simply says, "If you don't get a face lift, then you're not going to make it." Every one of these churches is about to face the dragon, the beast, and the harlot. If they are not pure, they will not last. You will not get into the kingdom of heaven with the kind of blemishes found in the present church. So he says, "Clean up, or don't expect to make it."

You can mirror each of these seven churches with a contemporary counterpart, likely in your own neighborhood. In other words, the problems they struggled with in the first century, churches struggled with in the fifth century, at the Revolutionary War, and today. These are the problems that still assail the people of God. There are basically four problems laid out in these seven churches. Let's take a look at them one at a time.

> Jesus says, "I know your deeds, your hard work, and your perseverance." Does that sound like your church?

LOST LOVE

The first problem comes from Ephesus. Chapter 2:1 reads: "To the angel of the church in Ephesus write . . . ." Time out! We must understand that the church of Ephesus was a fabulous congregation. It was, at that time, about forty years old. They had a string of famous preachers as long as your arm, including none other than Paul the apostle, Apollos, Timothy, Tychicus, John the apostle, Aquila and Priscilla. And according to one tradition, even Mary, Jesus' mother, lived there. It was a great congregation, the envy of other preachers.

Jesus says, "These are the words of him who holds the seven stars in his right hand and walks among the seven golden lampstands." What a reminder! In spite of the mess we're in, he is the ever-present High Priest. We had better pay attention.

"I know your deeds." Usually when a child hears a parent say "I know your deeds," that is not a happy phrase. For a good child, however, those words are sweet music! The church of Ephesus is like a good child. They are in for kudos and they know it. *Here is what Jesus says, "I know your deeds, your hard work, and your perseverance." Does that sound like your church?* We work hard; we persevere; we stick to it. Some can even relate when Jesus says, "I know that you cannot tolerate wicked men, that you have tested those that

21

THE SEVEN CHURCHES OF REVELATION 2-3

CHURCHES	PICTURE OF JESUS	PRAISE	REPROACH	PUNISHMENT	PROMISE
Ephesus	Holds 7 stars, walks among the 7 lamps	Hard work, perseverance, identify & intolerant of wicked men & false teachers	Forsaken first love — remember & repent	Remove lamp which is in the paradise of God	Eat from the tree of life
Smyrna	First and last, dead and rose	Affliction and poverty, slander, therefore faithful			Crown of life and not hurt by the second death
Pergamum	Has a sharp, double-edged sword	Remain true amidst Satan's throne	Teaching of Balaam & Nicolaitans; sexually immoral and eat foods sacrificed to idols — repent	Come and fight with the sword of my mouth	Hidden manna, white stone, new name known only by those who receive it
Thyatira	Son of God, blazing eyes, feet of bronze	Deeds, love, faith, service, perseverance, growth	Tolerate Jezebel, sexually immoral, and eat foods sacrificed to idols —repent	Bed of suffering, kill children according to your deeds	Authority over the nations
Sardis	Holds 7 spirits and 7 stars	A few are unsoiled	Dead and incomplete deeds — wake up, remember and repent	Come like a thief	Walk with Christ, dressed in white, name in the book of life (acknowledged by God)
Philadelphia	Holy and true, key of David, what he opens no one shuts	Kept word and not denied Jesus			Make false Jews acknowledge them, keep them from trial, make them a pillar, get a new name — God's
Laodicea	Amen, faithful, true, ruler of God's creation		Lukewarm and poor — buy gold, white clothes and salve (= repent)	Spit you out	Table fellowship with Jesus; reign with Jesus on a throne

claim to be apostles but are not, and have found them false. You have persevered and have endured hardships for my name, and have not grown weary." Folks, look in the mirror. For many, this is your home church — good deeds; good folk.

Remember the long walks and talks with Jesus? Where has all that gone?

But be careful! This next line will cut you. "Yet I hold this against you: You have forsaken your first love. Remember the height from which you have fallen! Repent and do the things you did at first." Our churches are filled with Marthas who busy themselves with table settings and communion clean-up but who have lost love for Jesus. Perhaps this is even you. You're in the church building several days a week, but the halls of your heart are empty. Are you tired of your prayers just bouncing off the ceiling? Can you remember when you used to crave the word of God? You used to take the Bible with you to work because at every break you just had to taste the bread of life. Remember how you had a string of people whom you were just dead set on telling about Christ? *Remember the long walks and talks with Jesus? Where has all that gone?*

Every once in a while married couples get into a rut where they don't communicate so well anymore. It just seems like nothing is easy. There is this uncomfortable distance and tension. That's like our relationship with Christ. He is our groom. So, you'd expect that the same kind of troubles that married couples have, Christians would have with their bridegroom. That is, indeed, the case.

So what advice should we give to married couples that sense that distance? Couples fall out of love because they have stopped doing the things that made them fall in love. It is really very simple. How much time did you devote to your spouse while you were dating? Most couples average about fifteen hours a week alone, just the two of them together. College students hear that and say, "Yeah, that's about right." Married couples hear that and say, "Huh?" How easily we forget. Nevertheless, if you would start spending the

23

same amount of time with your spouse now that you did back then, you would be just as romantic as you were back then. If you would spend the same amount of time talking as you did back then, you would have the same pizzazz as you did back then. It's really no great mystery. Obviously this is not a marriage manual. But since our relationship with Christ is compared to a marriage, this illustration is simply a way to see what it will take to rekindle our love for Christ.

The advice here in chapter two is pretty simple: "Remember the height from which you have fallen! Repent and do the things you did at first." *What were you doing as a new believer? Do it again.* Pick up your Bible and read it. Carve out some time for private prayer. Be faithful to the church when she meets together. Get involved in a ministry of compassion. Tell your friends and your family about your faith. None of this is difficult. All of it is essential. Please don't trivialize the loss of our passion for Christ. The church is about to encounter the dragon, the beast, and the harlot. We have zero chance for survival without a zealous love for Jesus.

FALSE TEACHING AND SEXUAL IMMORALITY

The second problem we face is embodied in the church at Pergamum as well as the church at Thyatira. Both had the same problem and their problem had two prongs. The first prong of the problem was false teachers.

In Pergamum, they had listened to the teachings of Balaam and in Thyatira they had listened to the teachings of Jezebel. Both Balaam and Jezebel teach the same thing. It goes like this: "If it feels good, do it." "It is expensive, but, Baby, you are worth it." "Be your own person." "Do your own thing." That sounds vaguely familiar. *The heresy of Balaam and Jezebel is self-worship — put yourself on the throne of your life.* Predictably, this theology leads to sexual immorality. That's the second prong.

What were you doing as a new believer? Do it again.

Satan is attacking the Church in its loins and winning. How many more deacons will lose their battle with sexual addictions? How many more elders

24

will fall to an affair? How many more preachers will split families and churches? How many more newscasts will bask in the shame of the church?

The heresy of Balaam and Jezebel is self-worship — put yourself on the throne of your life.

Jesus says in verse 13, "I know where you live — where Satan has his throne." We are living in a corrupt society just like Pergamum, where the billboards and the media are seducing us daily into this godless, heretical philosophy to feed ourselves and indulge in sensuality. It's obvious why we do this. It is all around us; this is Satan's territory. No one in Pergamum or Thyatira thought it strange to live in and for the flesh any more than they do in Las Vegas or San Francisco. Yet our deeds of darkness are not hidden from God. He notices. More than that, he *will* hold us accountable for the way we live.

If you are involved in fornication, Jesus sees and he cares. If you are involved in adultery or pornography, Jesus sees and he cares. If you are letting your casual conversation cross lines of familiarity, if you are letting casual touch linger beyond its innocence, Jesus sees and he cares. More than that, he is angry and perfectly capable of doing something about it. You may not have crossed that final line yet, but you are racing to get there just as fast as you can so that you can stand as close as you can, without *of course* falling over the edge. Be careful. Be wise. Be frightened.

If you have ears to hear, listen to what Jesus says about this Jezebel: Verse 22, "I will cast her on a bed of suffering, and I will make those who commit adultery with her suffer intensely, unless they repent of her ways." You had better get out of her bed or you will be in the same boat as she.

Jesus gives us this warning, but he also gives us this promise from verse 17, "He who has an ear, let him hear what the Spirit says to the churches. To him who overcomes, I will give some of the hidden manna. I will also give him a white stone with a new name written on it, known only to him who receives it." Sometimes as Christians we feel like we are

25

missing out on some of the sensual gratification of our society. The fact is we're not missing much. Our bridegroom adores us. He wishes for us the very best. So if Jesus calls us to forego some sensual pleasures, it is only because He has something better in store.

He hints at that in verse 17 when he says, "I will give you hidden manna." There is a source of nourishment and refreshment beyond what we can imagine. Be patient, Jesus will provide everything we need. You make him your only lover and he will make it worth your while.

DEAD, DEAD, DEAD

The third problem that the Church faced is in Sardis, chapter 3. "To the angel of the church in Sardis write: 'These are the words of him who holds the seven spirits of God and the seven stars. I know your deeds; you have a reputation of being alive, but you are dead. Wake up! Strengthen what remains and is about to die . . . .'" Have you ever been to a church where you wanted to pray, "Oh, Dear God, please let something happen here that is NOT printed in the bulletin!"? In the name of DIGNITY we stifle worship, fellowship, and service. We mustn't do anything to disturb our neighbor, you know. What a crock!

How can it be that a church would have a reputation for being boring?! If we truly understood the message of Christ, if we paid attention to half the words in the songs we sing, we would look like a special education class of ADHD kids, or a stadium full of sports fans. Excitement, NOT deadness, should characterize our fellowships.

> If we really see this majestic high priest, it would be very difficult for us to keep our seats and impossible to hold our tongues.

Yet we come to church and sing, "Blessed Assurance" like a funeral dirge! The church is the last place on earth we ought to be bored. Granted, not everyone expresses their excitement in the same way. I'm not suggesting a pep rally after communion. But I am suggesting that *if we really see this majestic high priest, it would be very diffi-*

26

cult for us to keep our seats and impossible to hold our tongues. How can we not get excited when we see our great high priest, the lamb that was slain for the sins of the world, the coming king and warrior God? My bridegroom is coming for me and that's worth getting excited about. You understand, a church that is dead is only dead because it has its eyes closed. You can't really see Jesus and remain passively "dignified."

It is not a sin to have money. It is a sin to love money; to trust money.

MATERIALISM

There is a fourth problem that the church faces. In 3:14-17 we read:

> To the angel of the church in Laodicea write: 'These are the words of the Amen, the faithful and true witness, the ruler of God's creation. I know your deeds, that you are neither cold nor hot. I wish you were either one or the other! So, because you are lukewarm — neither hot nor cold — I am about to spew you out of my mouth. You say, "I am rich; I have acquired wealth and do not need a thing." But you do not realize that you are wretched, pitiful, poor, blind and naked.

So they had a little too much money. No big deal, right? Perhaps you noticed that Laodicea is the only church about which Jesus had nothing good to say. The danger is that most of our American churches look more like Laodicea than any of the other six. We have money coming out our ears. *It is not, of course, a sin to have money. It is a sin to love money. It is a sin to trust money.* The problem with trusting money is that it is so deceptive. You are comfortable the entire time you are doing it without ever realizing just how far away from God you really are.

If you don't believe me, just answer these three questions: (1) Can you honestly pray the Lord's prayer? Oh sure, we do OK for most of it. But we get stuck when we get down to the part where it says, "Give us today our daily bread." How can we seriously make that petition with a freezer full of food and a pantry full of snacks? Do you really need God's provision of food *today*? (2) If the Holy Spirit were to suddenly cease to exist in this moment, how long would it take you to notice? What do you rely on him for, really? (3) *If God stepped away from your church and decided never to visit again, how many of your programs would go on undisturbed?* Would the choir still sing? Would your morning worship services be noticeably different? Would the youth programs suffer?

Do you see? Money makes us feel like we don't need God. It makes us trust in our own resources and our own abilities, without realizing just how inadequate we are to provide for our own needs. What can money really do? Ask a father who loses a child in an automobile accident what money can do. Ask a woman who has just been abandoned by her husband what money can do. Ask a doctor who has just diagnosed himself with terminal cancer what money can do. Can it bring back a loved one? Can it buy health or peace? Can it assure that our children will grow up to be godly or well adjusted? We need God so desperately. Money clouds our minds to think that we are self-sufficient. Yet every once in a while life implodes and there is nothing we can do about it because we have trusted in the wrong thing. We have served the wrong master with our time and attention.

Jesus stands at the door and knocks (3:20): "Here I am! I stand at the door and knock. If anyone hears my voice and opens the door, I will come in and eat with him, and he with me." So he stands out there and knocks, wondering if anyone inside hears him. He knocks, wondering if anyone inside sees him. The great High Priest is outside our door. Do you see him? Do you need him? Open the door and receive him. O Church of God, O Bride of Christ, be beautiful for your groom.

> If God stepped away from your church and decided never to visit again, how many of your programs would go on undisturbed?

REFLECTING ON LESSON TWO

1. As a group, look through the chart on p. 22. Which of the seven churches is most like yours?

2. Come up with three practical guidelines for simplifying your life so that you could make time to rekindle your first love.

3. Take time to pray, right now, for each person in the group, that they would be sexually pure. Pray for each marriage, each single person. Pray for your preacher, elders, and other church leaders. If you personally are struggling in this area, vow to God that you will confess your danger to a spiritual leader within 48 hours.

4. Is your church boring? Why? What can you do about it without splitting the fellowship? Let's not ask, "How can we jazz up worship?" but rather, "How can we help people see the great high priest?"

5. How did you answer the three questions on pp. 27-28?

6. Brainstorm as a group to come up with a list of ten things which could be done by families in your church to help them trust in God about money.

3

A BLUEPRINT FOR WORSHIP

So how does one go about dodging a dragon? What must we do when we are about to face the unholy trinity of the dragon, the beast, and the harlot? Step #1 is to get a clear view of Jesus (Ch. 1). Step #2 is to repent of our sins, to give the bride a face-lift (Chs. 2-3). Step #3, here in Revelation 4-5, is to worship God. *Worship doesn't just thrill the heart of God. It transforms the minds of men.* We need it, not just for our devotional amusement, but for our spiritual survival. Through worship, we recognize that God is on the throne. Through worship we understand that he, and he alone, can save us from our tribulation, and that in fact, it is not such a big deal for him to do so. Our tribulation, so ominous from our perspective, is minuscule in God's grand scheme. Worship opens our eyes to God's vastness. We see clearly from our knees God's ability to sustain us.

Perhaps you remember the story of Hezekiah from Isaiah 36. The evil Sennacherib was threatening to decimate Jerusalem. In fact, he sent Hezekiah a letter which read:

> This is what the great king, the king of Assyria, says: On what are you basing this confidence of yours? You say you have strategy and military strength — but you speak only empty words. On whom are you depending, that you rebel against me? Look now, you are depending on Egypt, that splintered reed of a staff, which pierces a

30

man's hand and wounds him if he leans on it! Such is Pharaoh king of Egypt to all who depend on him. And if you say to me, "We are depending on the LORD our God" . . . . The LORD himself told me to march against this country and destroy it.

> Worship doesn't just thrill the heart of God. It transforms the minds of men.

This letter was intimidating. It was devastating! Hezekiah's kingdom is on the brink of disaster. God's people are on the edge of extinction. So what does Hezekiah do? He takes the letter to the temple of the Lord and opens it up as if he were inviting God to read it. He prays,

"O LORD Almighty, God of Israel, enthroned between the cherubim, you alone are God over all the kingdoms of the earth. You have made heaven and earth. Give ear, O LORD, and hear; open your eyes, O LORD, and see; listen to all the words Sennacherib has sent to insult the living God. . . . Now, O LORD our God, deliver us from his hand, so that all kingdoms on earth may know that you alone, O LORD, are God" (Isaiah 37:16-20).

Hezekiah's in trouble. Yet instead of cowering in his prayer closet he's worshiping God in the temple. We are tempted to think that such times of distress are times for action, not times for worship. Yet our most desperate hours are precisely the times we need worship most. It was only after Hezekiah had placed God on the throne that he could get a proper perspective on his personal crisis. Furthermore, the battles we face are child's play for the God who created the heavens and the earth. Coming out of worship, when we ask for personal protection, it is for the purpose of God's greater glory, not our personal comfort. From the throne-room we see things differently. We tend to be much smaller than we estimate, and God tends to be much bigger.

Back to Revelation 4. As the chapter opens, someone left a door open in heaven. John senses that he doesn't belong. Yet he is invited up, so he enters. The things he saw! There was a throne with someone sitting one it. Its occupant is too obvious to identify. So John just describes him. He is pictured as jasper, carnelian, and a rainbow. Jasper is a precious stone that looks like an emerald. Carnelian is another jewel that looks like a ruby. A rainbow, well, I'm sure you've seen one. However, this rainbow is different. Instead of hues of reds and blues, this one was primarily green.

This is an awfully strange picture of God. What does it mean? In order to see the portrait clearly, we need to step back and breathe deeply rather than stepping forward and squinting. In other words, we need to see the big picture rather than counting brush strokes. There is likely little significance in each stone but a powerful message in the portrait as a whole. So what do we see when we step back? First, we notice that each stone is of great value. At the worth of God we say, "Wow." Second, we notice that each description is very beautiful. At the loveliness of God we say, "Ooh." Third, we notice these items are translucent, as if there were no closed closets in the throne room. At the openness of God we say, "Oh." *God is the "Wow, Ooh, Oh" of heaven. It is a breathtaking event to actually see a vision of God.*

Just about the time John catches his breath, he sees that God is not alone. He is surrounded by twenty-four elders. These are the rulers of God's people. Whether they are the twelve patriarchs with the twelve Apostles, or some other notable presbytery makes little difference. These are the guys with authority, power and dignity. They surround God in his throne room, garbed in white, decorated with golden crowns. They are accompanied by nature's big band and fireworks (4:5). God oozes power that shakes out in earthquakes and lightning storms. It would be quite magnificent if it weren't so overwhelming. Next to the twenty-four elders are the seven spirits of God, likely a cryptic description of the Holy Spirit (cf. 1:4-5; 5:6). John is distanced from all the action by a sea of glass. I suspect that was the only comforting part of this vision for John.

We're still not done. There were also some very strange looking creatures. The four of them, or at least their cousins, made an earlier appearance in

God is the "Wow, Ooh, Oh" of heaven. It is a breathtaking event to actually see a vision of God.

Isaiah 6. These mutants have eyes all over their bodies and three sets of wings. In turn, they had the head of a lion, an ox, a man, and an eagle. Frankly, this is a bit bizarre. What's the point? Very simply, the point is not what they look like but what they do. These creatures that span the gamut of the wild kingdom shout at the top of their lungs: "Holy, holy, holy is the Lord God Almighty, who was, and is, and is to come." Their task is to worship God in perpetuity.

> All of our accomplishments and kudos are for God's greater glory.

The elders take their cue from the creatures. Whenever they cry out, the elders bow down. They remove their crowns and say, "You are worthy, our Lord and God, to receive glory and honor and power, for you created all things, and by your will they were created and have their being." In heaven, even our crowns, the symbol of victory, authority, and accomplishment, only have value insofar as they bring honor to God. *All of our accomplishments and kudos are for God's greater glory.*

When the Lamb makes his appearance in chapter 5 it is a repeat performance. The four living creatures and the twenty-four elders sing a new song: "You are worthy to take the scroll and to open its seals, because you were slain, and with your blood you purchased men for God from every tribe and language and people and nation. You have made them to be a kingdom and priests to serve our God, and they will reign on the earth" (5:9-10). Then a ton of angels join in. There are so many they have to be counted in groups of ten thousands. They raise the rafters of heaven singing: "Worthy is the Lamb, who was slain, to receive power and wealth and wisdom and strength and honor and glory and praise." This chain reaction triggers all of creation, every breathing being in heaven, on earth and under the earth, even those in the sea, to sing: "To him who sits on the throne and to the Lamb be praise and honor and glory and power, for ever and ever." The four living creatures punctuate their worship with a final "Amen" and the elders prostrate themselves before the throne.

We have just taken a whirlwind tour of creation. We've seen representatives from every corner of the galaxy. There have been the leaders of God's people, the spiritual entities of heaven, the angels, the creatures of the earth and sea. What are they doing? Don't miss this marvelous message: *All created beings, when they see God for who he is, praise him with all they are.*

APPLICATION

The nature of worship. There are two great travesties concerning worship in our churches. First, we have equated worship with music. Music is a marvelous tool for worship. It is not, however, the only tool. When music is exclusively equated with worship, two bad things happen. First, we miss out on a lot of other wonderful tools that help us worship God. For example, we might miss bodily posture, silence, meditation, Bible reading, drama, architecture, fasting, prayer, journaling, etc. Each of these can accomplish things in us that the tool of music cannot touch. Second, and more dangerous, is equating worship with an action rather than an awareness. Old Testament worship basically consisted of what was done in the temple. There were sacrifices, prayers, washings, incense, etc. As long as you jumped through the right hoops, you had worshiped. The Greek word used to describe that kind of worship is *latreuo*, also translated as service. This kind of worship describes what we do in God's presence.

The New Testament, however, calls for a different kind of worship. Jesus put it this way, "God is spirit, and his worshipers must worship in spirit and in truth" (John 4:24). This kind of worship is described as *proskyneo*. Originally the word meant "to kiss toward." It is the picture of a crowd blowing kisses to a king or kneeling before him kissing his ring. By the time the N.T. was written, however, this word came to mean, "To bow before" or "to show abeyance." Worship, in its essence, then, is showing reverence to God. It is not what we do, but what we are aware of. You know you have worshiped when you recognize who God is and suddenly

All created beings, when they see God for who he is, praise him with all they are.

34

become aware that you are in his presence. So how can you know if you have worshiped? That is the second great travesty in our contemporary evangelical worship.

The direction of worship is not optional. It always has as its object and subject the person of God.

For many of our churches, riddled with an entertainment mentality, the barometer of worship is how I feel when I walk out the doors. Did I get fed? (Translated: Do I feel warm and fuzzy?) For other churches worship is gauged in much the same way as an aerobic workout. That is, how much movement was there and did I feel the pulse of the drums. Don't misunderstand, the style of the worship is not the issue. That is open to great diversity and personal preference. *But the direction of worship is not optional.* When we focus inward, we cannot, by definition, worship. Worship is always upward. *It always has as its object and subject the person of God.* Notice here in Revelation 4, God is the centerpiece of the throne room and in chapter 5, Jesus accompanies him in the spotlight. All these other entities face the dynamic duo and focus their attention on them. That's why it is fair to say that you have not worshiped until you get a clear vision of God. So we ask again, how does one know when (s)he has worshiped? Very simply: Did you see God? Were you aware of who he is and what he has done? If you were, you likely felt more fear than comfort, more heat than warmth.

No one who ever had been in the presence of God walked away and casually quipped, "What a blessing!" Daniel, Isaiah, Ezekiel, and John, to a man, when they saw God, fell down as though dead. Why? Because God is awesome, in the truest sense of the word. And there is not a great deal of difference in being awe*some* and being aw*ful*. While we don't fear condemnation, we are terrified at God's person. It's not that we are afraid he's going to beat us up, but he is just so big he's striking. It's kind of like a lightning storm. We jump at each flash, not so much for fear of being struck, but because it is just so striking. So it is with God. *When we suddenly realize that we are in the presence of omnipotence, we begin* *to feel small, polluted and unworthy.* These emotions are about as accurate a barometer of worship as you'll find.

The object of worship. In chapter five Jesus joins the Father in the center of the throne. They stand side by side as equals. Twice in Revelation John tries to worship an angel and is rebuffed both times. But Jesus allows all heaven and earth to exalt him as the eternal God without even a little quibble.

Indeed, Jesus robed himself in flesh for some thirty-three years. During our closest contact Jesus looked a lot like us. However, you mustn't let the disguise fool you. Prior to the incarnation he was the Eternal Word of God. Since then he is the Lion/Lamb Lord. Heaven praises Jesus every bit as much as they praise the Father. Jesus Christ is God and a worthy object of our worship.

The purpose of our worship. Worship probably does more good than we could enumerate. Nevertheless, two things stand out in this text. First, we notice the crowns of the elders (4:10). These represent victory and reward. These testify to positions of authority and a life well-lived. But when God gets praised, the crowns come off and are laid before the throne because he alone is worthy of recognition.

So, one of the things that worship does for us is to put recognition in its proper place. If we are to receive a crown in heaven it will serve only as an object of worship to God. All my accomplishments, are stored for one grand moment when I can lay them down at the throne. Here's my confession. I hope my crown is huge. I multiply my efforts to make it so, but not for self-aggrandizement. It is the desire of my life to get to heaven, bow before God, lay down a great big crown so that all heaven will come to its feet and say, "Now that's a gift worthy of the King." A life well lived is perhaps the greatest venue for the worship of God.

If we can place God on the throne in our worship, then the second purpose of worship will undoubtedly be accomplished. That is, we will be comforted in our affliction. Like Hezekiah, once

> When we suddenly realize that we are in the presence of omnipotence, we begin to feel small, polluted and unworthy.

36

you understand who God is, your enemy looks pretty puny. Once you get a glimpse of God, you see that he still occupies the throne, he is still in control. He is good and won't let you be destroyed through the tribulation. Worship is where we come to grips with both our enemy and our advocate. It is here we see clearly, here where faith is birthed, here where hope is kindled. Worship, then, is our first line of defense against the onslaught of the evil one.

REFLECTING ON LESSON THREE

1. How does worship help us encounter the trials of life?

2. As a group, come up with a definition for worship.

3. What are some of the "tools" for worship that you have not been utilizing that you would like to try?

4. Explain what it means to have worship focused upward rather than inward. What implications does this have for your own personal corporate worship?

5. Describe for the group a time when you clearly saw God. Where were you? What were you doing? What helped you see him? Can we reproduce any of this in our corporate church services?

6. What trials are you facing? How would a clear view of God on his throne help comfort you in those afflictions?

4

HOW DO WE HANDLE SUFFERING AS SAINTS?

We have all heard the stories. Those valiant saints of old held their ground in the face of lethal opposition. In A.D. 156, the aged saint Polycarp, was threatened with death if he would not deny Christ. He responded, "Eighty-six years have I served Christ and he never wronged me. How can I now speak evil of my king and savior?" Ignatius faced the Emperor Trajan. Rather than recant he called for the executioner, saying, "May I enjoy the wild beasts prepared for me . . . come fire, come cross, come crowds of wild beasts; come tearings and manglings, wracking of bones and hacking of limbs; come cruel tortures of the devil; only let me attain unto Jesus Christ."

Stories of valiant martyrs are inspiring. But the reality of human suffering is a bit more grueling. The raw fact is that Christians are still being killed for their faith. Indeed, there have been more Christian martyrs in the twentieth century than all others combined. In 1900 there were an estimated 35,000 martyrs. By 1991 it had increased to over 260,000. There have been more than ten thousand Christians killed every year since 1950. Today, more than twenty-five percent of Christians around the world are part of an "underground church." One out of every two hundred Christians living today can expect to die for their faith. In over 180 countries Christians have laid down their lives for their faith.

In Uganda, some 400,000 Christians died, fled the country or disappeared under Idi Amin. Christians were imprisoned and slaughtered by the thousands under the communist regimes of the U.S.S.R. and China. In many Moslem countries, such as in the Sudan, Christian women are sometimes raped so that they will bear Moslem children if they refuse to deny Christ. Children of Christians have been kidnapped and sold into slavery or prostitution, some of them for as little as $15. Gruesome stories can be multiplied. The bottom line is that Christians today around the world are suffering.

Whether your suffering is big or small, the principles for dealing with it are basically the same.

If God is good, he would not want saints to suffer. If God is all-powerful, surely he could do something about it! This creates quite a theological dilemma when good people suffer bad things. That's why Revelation 6 & 7 is so relevant. It deals with this very real and difficult issue.

Suffering is a strange thing. Mine is always worse than yours. And someone else's is always worse than mine. Yet *whether your suffering is big or small, the principles for dealing with it are basically the same.* Whether it is war or cancer, martyrdom or losing a friend these chapters help us understand what in the world God is doing. It is generally true that the greater our suffering, the more likely we are to understand what Jesus is trying to tell us with these very strange pictures. Yet even if our suffering doesn't come close to others', even though it may not reach biblical proportions, this text still has a message of hope for us.

Why does God allow his children to get beat up in the midst of a bad world? Watch. As we open chapter 6 of Revelation, the Lamb is opening up a scroll. Every time he opens one of the seals, something bad happens. With the first four seals come four horses. The first horse is white. A rider is mounted on its back. In his hand is a bow and on his head is a crown. This rider symbolizes military conquest.

The second seal pops open and out rides a second horse.

Everywhere there is military conquest this second horse follows. It is a red horse. Its rider has in his hand a long sword besmeared with blood. This is, unfortunately, not an uncommon picture for us. Ever since television cameras have opened up Vietnam for us, we have seen bloodshed as a result of war. In living color we've seen gaping wounds and live executions. If you are accustomed at all to watching the news, this picture is all too familiar.

The third seal pops off and out walks a black horse. This black horse also accompanies every war that's ever been fought. *When military conquest overshadows a country, people begin to die and economic structures crumble. The result is often famine.* We have seen at least one too many pictures from Compassion International of little children with bloated bellies. We are almost desensitized to it. It is such a common picture, we too easily forget the horror of the reality behind the portrait.

The fourth horse comes out. This one is pale. There is nothing in his hand, but Hades follows in his wake. Along with Hades, he has a parade of caskets and mourners and funerals.

All this is not a description of what will take place. Nor is this what *did* take place. This is a description of what always takes place. It does not surprise us that people die in war, that bad men go out through military conquest and kill people, that children starve as a result of war. There is nothing new in all of that. What comes next, however, is shocking. When the fifth seal pops open (v. 9), under the altar of God we see the slain martyrs. God's own people get caught in the cross fire of bad men's war. We cry out with the martyrs in verse ten: "How long, Sovereign Lord, holy and true, until you judge the inhabitants of the earth and avenge our blood?" Have you never asked that question? "God, how long are you going to let this go on?" How long will Bosnia take place? How long will South Africa escape your wrath? How long will China get away with human atrocities?! "How long, O

> With military conquest, people begin to die and economic structures crumble. The result is often famine.

40

Lord, before you begin to avenge the blood of your own people?"

"God, why do you allow bad things to happen to good people?" is a misguided question. It is misguided for at least three reasons. First, people aren't that good. Granted, it is the Lamb that pops open these seals. It is God who allows wars to take place. His sovereign will often ordains it. Nonetheless, *the bulk of human suffering is not because God desired it or caused it but because we live in a world where people are mean, selfish and cruel.* If you are suffering today (and there is a pretty good chance that you are), don't blame it on God. It may just be that you are living in a world that is broken and cursed, a world that you helped to fashion.

> The bulk of human suffering is not because of God but a world where people are mean, selfish and cruel.

Second, this is a misguided question because not only are people in general not very good, if we read chapters 2 & 3 correctly, the church isn't even that good. There is evil in the church that must be purged. That's what verse 11 is all about: "Then each of them were given a white robe, and they were told to wait a little longer." How do you think they got their white robes? Was it not through the very martyrdom they suffered? Sometimes the best way to grab hold of purity is through pain. Have you not noticed that? Most of us are just stubborn enough not to get off dead center until God gives us a swift kick when we bend over to tie our shoes. It is often in the midst of this pain that our greatest growth comes. So when we are suffering (and if you are not now you probably will be soon), perhaps the question we need to ask is this: "What does my wardrobe look like? Do I have anything white to wear to the wedding?" If not, this period of suffering may be a great time in your life. It is, perhaps, a necessary prerequisite to the Second Coming of Christ.

There is a third reason why this is a misguided question. We ask, "Why doesn't God avenge the blood of the martyrs?" Revelation responds, "He is!" That's what the first four horses are all about. God is punishing the wicked in our world.

The problem is, Christians just get caught in the cross fire. Look at these next few verses: "I watched as he opened the sixth seal. There was a great earthquake. . . ." Now we must listen with Jewish ears. In prophetic vocabulary, earthquakes typically talk about God's judgment. God is judging the wicked. Look at who he judges: "The sun turned black like sackcloth . . . the whole moon turned blood red, and the stars in the sky fell to earth . . . ."

After reading these verses, there is no need to look to the sky for galactic turmoil. Again, these verses are not predicting what is about to take place but are describing what always takes place in the midst of war. Several times in the O.T. we run across these same kinds of symbols — the sun is darkened, the moon is turned to blood and stars fall from the sky. In those places, the prophets are not talking about literal astronomical events but the fall of powerful nations. In Isaiah 13, these very same words are used to describe the fall of Babylon. In Isaiah 24, these same kinds of words are used to describe the fall of Tyre. In Ezekiel 32, Egypt takes a tumble. And in Matthew 24 they are applied to Jerusalem. What happens when men go to war? Those who cause the war often get dethroned. Listen to it, chapter 6, verse 15: "The kings of the earth, the princes, the generals, the rich, the mighty, and every slave and every free man hid in caves and among the rocks of the mountains." They will get what they deserve, often through war, ultimately on judgment day. In the meantime, God's full wrath against the wicked must be stayed. Here's why. Between the kings running to the rocks and the four horsemen, there are Christians getting killed. God's ear is not deaf to that. *He will not allow his chosen to suffer beyond their capacity to bear it.*

Why do we demand of God: "Do something about all these evil people in the world!"? What do you expect him to do? Send a flood? If he does, there are Christians in the middle of it. How about an earthquake? There are still Christians in the middle of it. A famine? A plague? Disease? There are innocent people in the midst of all the

God will not allow his chosen to suffer beyond their capacity to bear it.

42

catastrophes that strike the earth. God cannot punish the wicked without Christians getting caught in the cross fire. Perhaps God could turn the world into a giant Nintendo and just start picking off pagans one by one. God could do that. But if he did some of the

You are not forgotten by God. You are precious to him.

unbelievers he would "zap" would be our family and friends who have not yet come to know the love of Christ. Do you really want God to do that? No matter how you slice it, when God wreaks vengeance on this earth, Christians get dinged. That is just part of the world in which we live.

That doesn't help very much, does it? Chapter six doesn't help us handle suffering because it is the underneath side of suffering. It is suffering from the view we can see. It is suffering from our side of experience. However, chapter seven is suffering from the view that only God can see. So he unveils chapter seven for us and allows us to see why these things are happening right now in our world.

How is God going to comfort a church in the midst of suffering? What words can possibly alleviate such pain? If you are in the throes of tribulation, try these three on for size:

The first word comes from 7:3. There are these four angels standing at the four corners of the earth. They are holding back the winds that are going to blow destruction across the earth. God's angel commands them, "Don't release those winds . . . UNTIL we put a seal on the foreheads of the servants of God." As we read of this seal throughout the rest of the N.T. it becomes clear that this is the Holy Spirit of God. What does this mean? Precisely this: You are not forgotten by God. He has inscribed himself on your soul. You are his property. He will, therefore, not allow anything devastating to happen to his property that is out of control. This is precisely what we need to know in the throes of suffering. You are not alone. *You are not forgotten by God. You are precious to him.*

You might feel like God doesn't understand. It may seem that he is far away. But that is an illusion only sustained by this transitory world. If you could just see it from God's perspective, even for a moment, you would see that his finger-prints are all over you.

Because we have the Holy Spirit, God has not forgotten us. More than that, he will not forget us. We are saved! Because of that simple fact, our souls are secure even if our bodies are brutalized. That may not take away the pain, but it does baptize it in hope.

The second word for suffering saints comes from 7:10-12:

> And they cried out in a loud voice: "Salvation belongs to our God, who sits on the throne, and to the Lamb." All the angels were standing around the throne and around the elders and the four living creatures. They fell down on their faces before the throne and worshiped God, saying: "Amen! Praise and glory and wisdom and thanks and honor and power and strength be to our God forever and ever. Amen!"

Where is God? He is on his throne! This earth may be going to hell in a handbasket but God is not going anywhere! He is where he has always been. Read it in chapter four. He is glorious and lifted up in all his power and might and splendor. Angels and elders surround him in his glory. He is in control. *Is your life out of control? Not if you're God's child! Never! At least not while God is on the throne.*

A third word for suffering saints comes from 7:16-17. As they praised God and his Lamb, out slips, almost involuntarily, this description of heaven. "Never again will they hunger; never again will they thirst. The sun will not beat upon them, nor any scorching heat. For the Lamb at the center of the throne will be their shepherd; he will lead them to springs of living water. And God will wipe away every tear from their eyes."

Is your life out of control? Not if you're God's child — never, while God is on the throne!

Your suffering is not going to last forever. It simply will not last. It is momentary against the backdrop of eternity. There may be no earthly end in sight for your suffering. That's why God gave us this vision of Revelation, so that we might be able to realistically evaluate life in the here and now. Through this revelation we are able to envision God's broad scheme and our ultimate destiny.

**Don't give up.
DON'T GIVE UP!
*DON'T
GIVE UP!!!***

Even if your suffering reaches the horrific heights of these graphic pictures in chapter six, you must remember these three words: You are marked by God, God is still on the throne and heaven is real. Here's the point: Don't give up because Satan is dogging you. Don't run away from the church. Don't abandon your Lord. Don't allow the dragon, the beast and the harlot to get the better of you, because God is going to get the better of them soon enough! *Don't give up. DON'T GIVE UP! **DON'T GIVE UP!!!***

REFLECTING ON LESSON FOUR

1. Why is it misguided to ask "Why does God allow bad things to happen to good people?" What are some appropriate responses to this question?

2. What valuable lessons in life have you learned through the school of suffering?

3. How are these images of the four horses, earthquakes, and galactic turmoil being played out in our own day?

4. Which of these words of comfort from chapter 7 is most helpful to you?

5. What kind of suffering in this world might Christians be exempt from because of the work of the Holy Spirit?

6. What things help you remember that God is still on his throne?

7. How does a vision of heaven practically help you through the trials here on earth?

5
F I V E

SUFFERING WITHOUT THE SAVIOR

If you think it's tough to suffer as a Christian, you ought to try suffering as a pagan! In the first cycle of sevens (ch. 6–7), Christians suffer the seals along with their non-Christian neighbors. This second cycle of sevens (ch. 8–9), however is different. The Bride of Christ is exempt from much of the stuff that assaults the world through the trumpets.

It goes something like this: The seventh seal is broken and all heaven stands in awe for a half an hour (8:1). Why? Because the seventh seal (as well as the seventh trumpet and the seventh bowl), represents the final judgment of God. The courtroom always sits in silence as it awaits the reading of the verdict. But the silence doesn't last long. Soon come the sounds of judgment: "peals of thunder, rumblings, flashes of lightning and an earthquake" (v. 5, cf. 4:5; 11:19; 16:18). All this would be too much to take, save the one note of comfort. That is, the angel of God delivers to his Majesty the prayers of the saints. God has listened to his church; she is secure through the judgment.

Suddenly the tape rewinds and we go through the cycle again. In other words, we move from heaven and the end of time, back to the earth and the time of tribulation. This time, however, we look at the suffering of the world from a differ-

47

ent angle. In the first round, we were looking at the tribulation through the lens of the church. In round two, we see it from the vantage point of the world. Here's what happens.

Seven angels make their appearance. They form a catastrophic brass band. Each has a trumpet to blow. The first verse is played by the first four trumpets. The tune they sound is called "natural disasters." The first trumpet destroyed a third of the earth, the second a third of the sea. The third did in a third of the earth's fresh water and the fourth a third of the heavens. The bad news is that Christians suffer these first four trumpets. Not only do we have to put up with the evil schemes of rotten men (6:1-8), we also suffer natural disasters right along with the wicked in this world. The good news, however, is this is the end of our suffering. From here on out, there is a marked difference (pardon the pun) in how the pagans suffer. Watch.

After the echo of the fourth trumpet fades, there appears in the sky an eagle. As one might suspect in a book such as this, the eagle talks, or more accurately, it screams. Its message is slightly less than pleasant: "Woe! Woe! Woe to the inhabitants of the earth, because of the trumpet blasts about to be sounded by the other three angels!" (8:13). Thankfully these woes are not something we have to worry about in the church. We may suffer in the world, but we are not cursed with the world.

WOE #1: PUNISHMENT IN THE WORLD

God is not blind to the evil in this world. He is not passively sitting back, winking at its transgressions. His punishment may not always be swift, but it is certainly sure. Sometimes it comes from the most unusual places. The fifth angel sounds a blast and a star shoots out of heaven. Now, we already know that stars represent angels, or more literally, messengers. Not all these messengers are good. We get a couple of clues, in fact, that this particular angel is bad news. First, he's going in the wrong direction. He's falling out of heaven. Second, he's opening up the Abyss. In case you haven't figured it out, nothing good

God is not blind to the evil in this world.

48

ever comes out of there. Buckle your seat belt, something bad is about to take place.

The lid comes off the Abyss. Smoke billows out and darkens the sky. Then a bunch of bugs come out of the clouds of smoke. They are locusts. *However, you'll not find these critters in your ordinary entomology textbooks.* These suckers are mutants! They have a sting like a scorpion, the appearance of horses, human faces and women's hair. They have the teeth of a lion and a breastplate of iron. The beat of their wings is deafening. But most frightening of all, they are organized by none other than Abaddon, that is, the destroyer angel in charge of the Abyss.

If you didn't know better, you'd think that John got into some mushrooms on Patmos. What in the world does this mean? What kind of picture is John trying to paint? If you think like a Jew, it is really not that difficult to figure out. If you lived in Palestine and ate a bad bowl of curds before you went to bed, and you had a scary dream, this would be just the kind of image your mind would concoct. You see, John is pulling into this picture all the things the Jews feared most: A locust plague, Parthian invaders, and wild animals such as lions and scorpions.

Locust plagues in the Middle East were fearsome. When you saw them coming, there was absolutely nothing you could do. They would settle on your crop and eat nearly every bit of vegetation and then just vanish as quickly as they came. Sometimes they left after a few hours, sometimes after a few days. But notice what John says about these locusts. They settle in for the kill. They stay for the full five months. Why five months? Because that is the life-span of the locust. In other words, as long as these guys are alive, they will torment unbelievers. They make life so miserable that death would be a blessing. Yet unbelievers aren't even granted the mercy of ending it all.

The Parthians, who lived to the far north of Israel, were fierce fighters. They specialized in swift cavalry tactics. They had long hair like women's hair, and they were merciless killers. Oddly, the Jews liked them, at least a little bit. The Parthians were the only ones who were any real threat to Rome. For that, the Jews appreciated them. Still, there is no love lost on these locusts. They are bad to the bone and they are in the face of those who do not have the seal of God on their forehead (v. 4)!

So what are these locusts? Well, seeing as how they are led by Satan and come up out of the Abyss, a likely guess is that they are demons. This makes a lot of sense too. Satan organizes his troops to wreak havoc on the earth . . . with God's permission, of course. He causes a lot of trouble with believers, no doubt, but his hands are really tied there. Think about it. *What tools does Satan have to work with? There are really only four: Accusation, death, deception, and intimidation.* If you are a believer in Christ, Satan has no more power of accusation over you (Rom 8:34). Nor does death hold any sting (1 Cor 15:54-57). All Satan can do is deceive and intimidate Christians. However, if you are in the Word of God, you are not easily duped. And if you are filled with the Holy Spirit, you're undeniably overpowering (1 John 4:4). There will be more on this to come in chapter 20, but suffice to say here that Satan's work with believers is radically curtailed.

Unbelievers, on the other hand, don't have such protection. Satan has almost free reign with those of his number. They are hounded by demons of deception who make their lives miserable. Some suffer psychological torment. Others are hooked to addictions that rob them of life, security, and integrity. Others are oppressed, some even possessed, by demons who control their minds and sometimes their bodies. That says nothing of the nightmares, the guilt, the secrets, the habits, the fear, or the shame. We are free from all this through the blood of Christ! Sure Christians suffer in this world. But praise be to God that we don't suffer like pagans. The first WOE is ended, a second is to come.

Satan works with four tools: accusation, death, deception, and intimidation.

50

WOE #2: THE FINAL BATTLE ON EARTH

> The choice is simple, but radical: Get on the right side of the battle line or die.

Are you surprised to come to the end of the world so early in the book? Don't be. It's come up already (6:12-17). And it will come up again several more times (8:5; 10:6-7; 11:15-19; 14:7, 14-20; 16:14-18; 19-22). What we're looking at here is a pattern, not a chronology. The pattern is simple: Evil runs rampant, so God tries to check it with ever increasing suffering (Woe #1). This contest comes to a head in a final decisive battle (Woe #2). This battle is followed by the end of the world and the final judgment (Woe #3).

At this point in the scenario, God is attempting one last time to call the wicked to repentance. (This battle will be better described in chapters 19 and 20). *The choice is simple, but radical: Get on the right side of the battle line or die.*

The warriors are difficult to identify. They are led by four angels. These four angels have been chained at the river Euphrates, a strategic location of the ancient world. They are ready to march in all directions with a militia of immense proportions. Here's the curious thing. These angels are clearly God's messengers, but they are not necessarily good angels. After all, did God ever chain up someone on his side? And the horses breathe smoke and sulfur and their tails are vipers (9:18-19). That sounds more like a demon than Michael or Gabriel! Again, we likely have demons destroying the people of the world. What is different, however, is that this time, they are not directed by Satan, but by God himself.

It is bad enough to find yourself under demonic attack. But to find yourself in a face-off with God is beyond frightening. Yet that is precisely the position of all who reject God's Son. In the end, unbelievers will find themselves struggling in a world oppressed by wicked men, subject to natural disasters and riddled with demonic influence. Worse than all this, however, they will also find themselves at odds with the creator and sustainer of the universe.

Please don't misunderstand, at this point, God's punishment is still redemptive. He's not out there zapping bad people because they made a few mistakes. He's calling people to repentance. Sadly, the saga ends without mass conversion. "The rest of mankind that were not killed by these plagues still did not repent of the work of their hands; they did not stop worshiping demons, and idols of gold, silver, bronze, stone and wood — idols that cannot see or hear or walk. Nor did they repent of their murders, their magic arts, their sexual immorality or their thefts" (9:20-21).

Why does God allow such suffering in this world? Because he is mean and nasty? On the contrary, God is not willing that any should perish but that all would come to repentance. True enough, but it's more than that. God is dead set on justifying himself. When judgment rolls around at the next trumpet blast, there will be no one who can say, "But I just didn't understand" or "I just wasn't given enough warning." By that time the battle lines will be set in stone, and God will have every right to let his anger flare.

SO WHAT?

Why would God take the time in such an important book as this to tell us what he is going to do with unbelievers? After all, this book is written to a decidedly Christian audience. Answer: Sometimes when Christians suffer, they are tempted to throw in the towel. After all, some were mistakenly told that Jesus was the answer to all their problems, only to find out that coming to Christ often creates problems that weren't there before.

This book reminds us that we mustn't give up the faith. Don't ever let go of Jesus Christ. Not only will there be a great reward for those who are faithful, there is great suffering for those who aren't. And lest someone think, "Yeah, I'll suffer later, but for the time being it will be better to live comfortably in this world. Besides, I may get lucky and repent before it is too late." No, no, a thousand

This book reminds us that we mustn't give up the faith. Don't ever let go of Jesus Christ.

times no. *Regardless of what a Christian goes through, it is better to suffer as a believer than to live as a pagan.* And the closer we get to the coming of Christ, the truer that becomes.

Regardless of what a Christian goes through, it is better to suffer as a believer than to live as a pagan.

Sometimes we are seduced into thinking that things are more comfortable in the world than in the church. Revelation reveals that this just is not so! We may suffer evil men's wicked schemes. We may even suffer from natural disasters. But when we put our head to the pillow at night, we need not fear death, feel shame, wrestle with remorse, carry guilt, search for hope, worry over our destiny or wonder about our destination. We don't have to dodge demons, live with locusts, run from horsemen, or cower under Satanic attack. More than all this, we don't have to face God in a contest of colossal proportions. In fact, he stands with us as our shield and first line of defense.

So you're suffering? Welcome to the club. Don't give up on God. True enough, he may, in fact, be the one responsible. But where else can you go for protection? Who else can heal? What else affords the comfort you long for? Unless you're prepared to fight against God, you had better stick with him.

REFLECTING ON LESSON FIVE

1. What are the three woes the world experiences from which the church is exempt? Give specific examples of how this principle plays out today.

2. If you, like John, were to pull together all the things that make up our nightmares into one horrific picture of Judgment, what would your Apocalyptic portrait look like? In other words, use your creative imagination to try to recreate an image that would do for us today what John's image of judgment did for his audience.

3. What are the four weapons of Satan (p. 50) and why are they powerless against Christians?

4. What is the pattern of suffering in this world — how do the three "woes" lead up to the judgment of God?

5. Is God in control of evil angels? How does that work? And what does that mean?

6. How is it that woe number two will ultimately justify God?

7. Why would God take the time in such an important book as this to tell us what he is going to do with unbelievers?

6
S I X

THE SPIRITUAL REALITIES BEHIND THE VEIL

On the average Sunday morning what do you see when you look around the church building? Probably some pews and a pulpit, smiling people all dressed up and toting Bibles. There may be a smattering of stained glass, flower arrangements and a baptistry. These are the kinds of things we can see with the naked eye.

However, what might we spy if the physical veil were drawn aside and we could see the spiritual realities invisible to this human plane? Perhaps there would be demons lurking in the corner, little imps spewing gossip. Perhaps puffs of sulfur would light from their nostrils as they launched half-truths in the minds of God's people. Maybe a few of them would carry addictions as they clung to people's ankles like chains or rode proudly on shoulders of unsuspecting victims. With leathery skin and wings like bats, they might flit about wreaking havoc in the church. We might also spy brawny angels in dazzling white surrounding children and widows. With wings unfurled and swords drawn they stand guard over the beloved of God. What would we see? These are merely imaginative descriptions. Nevertheless, the spiritual forces behind the veil are very much real and we deal with them daily. If only we could see them, we might take more seriously the battle we're in.

That's why chapters 11–13 are so important. These visions open our eyes to the real battle we face, the real characters with whom we wage war. Each chapter describes our spiritual struggle from a different angle. In chapter 11 we view it from the perspective of the church. Chapter 12 looks at it from heaven's vantage point. And chapter 13 sees it from the lens of the world.

FROM THE PERSPECTIVE OF THE CHURCH

Like Ezekiel of old, John is told to measure the temple (Ezek 40). In other words, this is a view of God's people, after all, the outer courts are excluded (11:1-2). This holy house of God will be pummeled by pagans for 42 months, that is 1,260 days, i.e., 3½ years. This is an account of the tribulation. If we were so inclined, we might look for a literal period of suffering. But certainly John's audience would echo back from their graves: "We've already been through the tribulation." How can we know that? Because 7:14 says so. Here we see some of the martyrs of old who have already gone through the great tribulation (7:14) and stand before the throne of God pleading on behalf of those still suffering (6:10). This is not to deny a period of intense suffering just before Jesus returns (1 Tim 4:1-5). But it is to say that *the term "tribulation" adequately describes what many Christians in all corners of the world have been going through since Jesus' ascension.*

Thus, 3½ likely has more to do with being an indefinite period of time than a literal reckoning of days. For John's audience, 3½ was the right symbol to represent the persecution of God's people. That's how long Elijah hid after causing a drought (James 5:17). That was the length of the Maccabean war waged against the evil Antiochus Epiphanes (June 168–Dec. 165 B.C.). That was the span of Jesus' own ministry between his baptism and his ascension. It was the period that shrouded Jerusalem when it was finally destroyed by the Romans (February A.D. 67–August 70). When these first

"Tribulation" describes what many Christians in all corners of the world have been going through since Jesus' ascension.

century Jewish Christians heard "3½," they would intuitively gasp, "Uh Oh! God's people are going to get it!" Perhaps there was (or will be) some specific, literal 3½ year period predicted here. Nevertheless, the principles in this passage span the course of church history. This is likely not what will take place but what always takes place when Christians suffer in this world.

> Elijah took a flaming taxi to heaven, and Moses was buried by the very hand of God.

Here's what happens. During this period of tribulation there are two witnesses. John borrows the image from Zechariah 4 to describe them as two lampstands and two olive trees. The lampstands, obviously, give light to the house of God. How do they give light? Well, they burn olive oil. So, since these lamps are connected to the olive trees with an umbilical cord, they can burn perpetually. Boy, do they ever burn! In fact, the word that comes from their mouth consumes its enemies like a dragon's breath. That's precisely how God described Jeremiah's preaching (Jer 5:14). These two extraordinary witnesses have the power of Elijah to shut up the sky and the power of Moses to turn water into blood (11:6). That is significant. Neither of these two men met death in an ordinary way. *Elijah took a flaming taxi to heaven, and Moses was buried by the very hand of God.* That's why the Jews expected these two eschatological figures to return as harbingers of the end.

So should we look for Moses and Elijah to tag team prior to Jesus' return? Probably not. Should we look for two other dynamic preachers who personify Moses and Elijah? Probably not. The number "two" represents a legal witness according to Mosaic law. So if we weigh the number rather than count it, we come up with an interpretation that looks something like this: The legal witness of God (in whatever form it takes), will have the power of the two greatest figures of biblical history. Their word will go forth perpetually as a light to God's people and a consuming fire for his enemies. The bottom line is that the preaching of the gospel through the church will be powerful in our world.

History has shown that the gospel has been powerful. It has pene-trated nearly every corner of our globe and permeated much of it. Yet Satan is not going to sit still long. He rises from the Abyss and attacks the witness of God. They lay slain in the street as all tongues and tribes gawk at their bodies in delight. For three and a half days they lay there. This is a pretty short period compared to the three and a half years they preached. Just when it looks like the Devil wins, God intervenes. He raises the witnesses back to life and punishes all who oppose them. There is a final battle, the second woe (vv. 13-14). The seventh trumpet is blown signaling the final judgment of God (vv. 15-19). Once again, we come to the end.

This is a parable of the church. Its message is pretty simple, really. The gospel is preached with victory and power. Satan opposes it with cruel and lethal force. God intervenes, crushing all his enemies and ushering in the final judgment. What does all this mean? Hang on just a little bit.

HEAVEN'S VANTAGE POINT

Chapter twelve opens and two figures loom large in the heavens. The first is a gargantuan woman. She is nearly nine months pregnant and robed with the sun. The child she is about to bear is the Messiah (v. 5). She is not little Mary, but all Israel. She is pursued by a second figure, a dragon. This dragon has seven heads (representing great authority), each with its own crown (representing victory and dominion). Speckled across his brow are ten horns (representing complete power). This is the Devil. He wages war in heaven and wreaks havoc among the angels. A third of the stars fall because of him, perhaps representing the angels who followed his rebellion. We rejoice that Michael and the good angels won the day and cast Satan to the earth. Problem: now the Devil is on the earth. That's where *we* live. And he is hot on our tails. He chases the woman into the desert. But God protects her for 1,260 days. This is the same picture as chapter 11 and the same 3½ years. It is simply seen from a different angle.

History has seen the gospel penetrate nearly every corner of our globe.

58

Things look bad for the woman. In fact, Satan spews a river that looks like it will overwhelm her. Just in the nick of time the earth itself opens up and swallows the river. The Devil is thwarted and a bit perturbed. We cheer until we realize that once he leaves off hounding the woman, he chases her offspring. Hey, that's us! Christians are under Satanic attack. If Michael and the good guys had trouble ousting him from heaven, what kind of chance do we have to survive his onslaught? The answer comes in 12:11. *We will not overcome. We have already overcome.* The battle is not up to us. It has already been fought and decisively won by Jesus' death blow on Calvary. So what does this parable mean? Hold on just a little bit.

> We *will* not overcome. We *have already* overcome.

THROUGH THE LENS OF THE WORLD

In chapter 13 we are introduced to two beasts. The first comes out of the sea. In Revelation, "sea" represents many peoples (cf. 17:1, 15). So this beast arises from the nations of the world. We also notice that he looks a lot like the Dragon. Both have seven heads and ten horns. The beast has three more crowns than the Dragon, but the difference is negligible. We look at the two of them side by side and say, "Like father, like son."

Each of the ten heads has a blasphemous name. And his mouth is no better; it too utters blasphemy. The beast is allotted 42 months to spout off. In other words, the whole time the two witnesses are preaching and the whole time the dragon is pursuing the woman, this beast is doing his thing. All of this is going on at once.

It gets worse. One of the heads incurs a fatal wound. Miraculously and unexpectedly the head survives. This captures the attention of the whole world. John likely had Nero in mind, and the legend of his resurrection from the dead. Others look for a yet future fulfillment in a specific governmental leader. But this much seems certain. There is a government which carries out Satan's program, deceiving the peoples of the earth. This first beast, however, doesn't operate alone. A second beast arises from the land. This one, instead of imitating the dragon, tries to imitate the lamb (13:11). This is enough to make any good Christian furious. How dare this beast act like he is the lamb! Nonetheless, open your eyes and you'll not have to look far to find false religions working in tandem with Satanic government for the purpose of leading people away from God. This second beast, through his miraculous signs, is primarily responsible for the success of the first.

So the question becomes: *Which government is the first beast and which false religion is the second? Answer: Take your pick.* Could I say it again? This *may* have a literal fulfilment in one particular government, but the principles of this text apply not only to what happened in John's day nor to what will happen before Christ returns, but to what always happens. This is the way our world operates! Look around at Iraq. You have a pagan government carrying out the Devil's program with the support of a false religion. You could look at the former U.S.S.R. supported by the religion of atheistic humanism. Try on for size Cuba, China, India, Bosnia, Ancient Rome, Babylon, Egypt or a host of others. You might even look to a nation that censors the Bible in her schools yet passes out condoms for free. A nation that kills more infants *in utero* every year than the lives it has lost in all its wars combined. A nation where pornography and perversion are protected by freedom of expression, but we mustn't offend anyone with a nativity scene on the steps of a courthouse. Oh dear God, have mercy on us; make our blind eyes see!

So what does this parable mean? Hold on just a little bit. That's right . . . that's what it means. You must hold on just a little bit longer. We live in a world where God's witnesses are slaughtered. We live on the earth where the woman's offspring are dogged by a dragon. We live among nations of false religions and Satanic governments. It's a tough place to live, but we'll not be here long. So, if we can just hang on for a little longer,

> **Which government is the first beast and which false religion is the second? Take your pick.**

we'll see the victory of God and the rescue of his children.

John says, "He who has an ear, let him hear. If anyone is to go into captivity, into captivity he will go. If anyone is to be killed with the sword, with the sword he will be killed. This calls for patient endurance and faithfulness on the part of the saints" (13:9-10). These words are borrowed from Jeremiah 15:2 and 43:11. They are God's warning to his people: "I have a program to carry out and there is nothing you can do to stop me. Some of you will get swept up in the punishment of the wicked. That's as it must be. But mark my words, when the exile is over, I'll make all things right." Some of the tribulation we suffer is simply God positioning Satan for a checkmate. As believers we get caught in the cross fire. This is how it must be according to God's sovereign plan. It is not because we are being punished but because Satan is. It is not because God hates us but because he hates wickedness. If we will but hold on, when the dust settles God will make all things right. In due time we will see just how right God is to allow what goes on in our world. Meanwhile, we will just have to wait for heaven. *If we hold on to Jesus, however, it will be well worth the wait.*

If we hold on to Jesus, it will be well worth the wait.

We should remember as well that the beast who blasphemes his been given a mouth and the 42 months in which to revile God. Who, pray tell, gave him his mouth? Who but God can? This is an incredible observation. God created the Devil, the government and the clock. He controls all three with sovereign precision. Satan is a wicked devil but he is still God's devil. Therefore, we mustn't let the adversities of life overwhelm us as if they were out of God's control. He is wise and he is good. If we can just hold on a little bit longer, we will see that with striking clarity.

Finally, we must deal with this mark of the beast (13:16-18). First of all, we must remember that this is not the first mark given in Revelation. The first was the mark of the Spirit given in 7:3. It was a spiritual mark, it was the character of God stamped on the believers' lives. Thus, our first guess about the mark of the beast is that it is the character of the Beast stamped on the lives of unbelievers. Some search for bar codes, Social Security numbers, or subdermal scanners. Yet in their search they miss the mark. For instance, many people would never allow their Social Security number to be put on their driver's license, but they will drive to movies that drip with the program of the beast. They would never think of getting a subdermal scanner put in their hand, but they pick up a tabloid at the checkout line that reeks of the world. We're scared to death of bar codes when we should really concentrate our caution on cable, Internet, gossip, slander, materialism and a host of other pagan ideals that we have baptized as acceptable Christian divergences. Wake up church! Rid yourself of the mark of the beast, this stench of the world that saturates our lives. This odor which we have become accustomed to is a toxin designed for our demise. If you want to dodge the dragon, you cannot afford to smell like him.

His mark, the mark of humanity, is not seen with the naked eye; it is adopted with raw passions. This 666 is the character and purpose of the Devil which inundates our society so much so that we can't even go to the market without being overwhelmed by it. It is this world's sensuality and arrogance, slander and selfishness, materialism and deceit. *We would do well to fear worldliness more than numeric tattoos.* We must wash our hands and face of any trappings of the Evil one. That's easier said than done in times of tribulation during these "3½ years." It all boils down to this: Do you see clearly the spiritual entities with whom we deal daily? Do you have faith? — Do you believe that God will defeat the dragon and the beast? We will be marked as property of one side or the other. You decide. Choose wisely.

We would do well to fear worldliness more than numeric tattoos.

REFLECTING ON LESSON SIX

1. What does "3½" likely represent? Where else have we encountered this 3½ year image?

2. Whom (or what) do you think these two witnesses represent? What role will they play in the church? How are they a "parable of the church" today?

3. What do the following symbols represent: seven, ten, heads, horns, crown, 1260 days, woman, dragon, beasts, sea?

4. The first beast imitates the dragon. Who does the second imitate? What role does each play in God's drama? Where and how do you see these two beasts at work today?

5. What does the phrase mean, "this is not what did take place or even what will take place but what always takes place"? Is this a fair way to look at Revelation? Does this view make the text more meaningful and relevant to you today?

6. What does the little injured head represent? And what does his recovery cause to happen?

7. What is the dominant message of these three chapters? How does the warning against the mark of the beast relate to this dominant message? Be honest about your own involvement with "666." Have you been marked by this world? And what steps will you take to purge yourself of this?

7

THE FINAL SEVENS

We come now to the seven last plagues (15) and the seven bowls of God's wrath (16). There's not a lick of difference between the two. Both are designed to punish God's enemies. Let's review. The first of the "sevens series" were the seals (ch. 6–7). They showed how men suffer on the earth from evil men's wicked schemes. As a result of the seals, the saints of God were sealed. The church stood victorious in a world of woe. Then came the seven trumpets, both natural and supernatural afflictions (ch. 8–9). Their purpose was to call men to repentance. Or perhaps more realistically, they provided an opportunity for wicked men to repent. When they don't repent, however, it demonstrates that God is just when he judges and punishes. They had every opportunity to turn to God. Therefore they have no excuse when God turns on them. (More on this in a moment). Now we come to the final cycle. These sufferings are not for purifying the saints. Nor are they for calling sinners to repentance. This is raw, unadulterated wrath, straight from the throne of God.

This is a chilling thought, not so much because of the fearsome anger of God, but because of our aversion to a God who has such a temper. We have pictured him as eternally patient. You know, the grandfather who rocks on the front porch doling out candy to the grandkids regardless of their mischief. This popular portrait of God is woefully errant. God does have a temper. And all our objections, philosophic or otherwise, won't undo the nature of God. Furthermore, *it is hardly realistic to imagine a God of love who is not also a God of wrath.* A mother whose child is in danger is more fearsome than a bear robbed of her cubs. A man whose lover is assaulted has a lethal zeal. It seems, therefore, that the greater the love, the greater the wrath. If that is true, then God's punishment of the wicked can be expected to match his love for the saints. Even John 3:17 is a necessary balance to John 3:16. Some can't believe in a God of love who punishes his enemies. The Bible can't picture a God of love who doesn't!

So there you have it. The sea of glass flares with the fire of retribution (15:2). Beside the sea are the saints. They hold harps in their hands and they begin to sing a song. It is a song patterned after Moses' song (Exod. 15). You remember. When Pharaoh's armies pursued the Israelites into the desert, they drowned in the sea. God's people stood on the opposite shore and sang a song of praise. This is the same scene, only it is heightened in heaven. This hymn to God is a victory ode extolling his power and holiness, both of which consume his adversaries.

Out of the heavenly temple march seven angels dressed like priests. They each have a bowl. It's not a soup bowl but rather the kind of bowl the ancients used for drinking wine. This picture is drawn from Jeremiah 25:15ff. There Jeremiah is commanded to curse all the countries who have waged war against God's people. Same song, final verse. The bowls of God's wrath are about to spill over on the nations of the world.

Several observations should be made about these bowls of wrath. First, they are a reenactment of the plagues of Egypt. Revelation is really the story of the Exodus, where God's people are liberated from bondage in this world. The exodus of Moses set the stage. By him God established a nation. Fifteen hundred years later another liberator came on the scene. Jesus freed us from our sin. Our memorial meal of communion is a Passover remembrance and a celebration of a newly established nation. By Jesus, God established a kingdom. Now, in the not-so-distant future, *God himself will liberate his people, and the ultimate exodus will finally be accomplished.* For the purpose of understanding this passage, it will be helpful if you keep one eye on Revelation and the other eye on Exodus.

Second, we should observe that the cycle of trumpets and the cycle of bowls are almost identical as the chart on the following page will show.

The difference between the judgments is that they get more severe the further into the book we go. They also get more deliberate. The first series of seals looked a lot like human travesty (albeit God-ordained). The second series of trumpets were natural and supernatural disasters, obviously ordered by God. This third series of bowls, however, comes directly from God's inner sanctum. Its effects are not partial (¼ or ⅓) like the first and second series of sufferings. The devastation of these bowls of wrath causes total annihilation.

Then, in the middle of the most severe cycle of judgment, heaven echoes the praise of God for these very acts of devastation. "'You are just in these judgments . . . for they have shed the blood of your saints and prophets, and you have given them blood to drink as they deserve.' . . . 'Yes, Lord God Almighty, true and just are your judgments'" (16:5-7). Is this Christian sadism? Are we really to believe that heaven celebrates the devastation of the earth? *At this point we can either change our view of God or rewrite the pages of Scripture.* His wrath is NOT antithetical to his kindness. Rather, it is essential to his holiness. He is a fool who demands God to love rebels above his own righteousness. And he is a double fool who believes he can enforce such a demand. All of our wishful thinking and politically correct platitudes will not alter the very nature of God even a little.

God himself will liberate his people, and the ultimate exodus will finally be accomplished.

A Comparative Chart of God's Judgments

	Seven Seals (Rev 6; 8) Cf. Zech 1:8-12; 6:1-8	Seven Trumpets (Rev 8–9; 11) Cf. Exod 8–9	Seven Bowls (Rev 16)
1	White Horse; rider with a bow War	Hail & fire mixed with blood ⅓ of the vegetation destroyed	Poured on the Earth Sores on those marked by the beast (Exod 9:10f)
2	Red Horse, rider with a sword Murder	Blazing mountain ⅓ of the sea, its creatures and ships	Poured on the Sea Everything in the Sea died (Exod 7:19ff)
3	Black Horse, rider with scales Famine	Falling star ⅓ of rivers and springs	Poured on rivers and springs Drinking water turned to blood
4	Pale Horse, rider named death Pestilence	Sun, moon & stars Loss of ⅓ of the lights	Poured on the Sun People scorched with fire
5	"How long, Lord?" Martyrs	"Star" opens the Abyss; Smoke and scorpion locusts come out; 5 months of the sting-sickness for those not sealed by God 1ST WOE IS PAST	Poured on the beast's throne His kingdom plunged into darkness; men gnawed their tongues and cursed God because of their sores.
6	Earthquake, Galactic turmoil Natural Disasters; Nations Overthrown; or Judgment	Release of the four angels at the Euphrates & 200 million troops ⅓ of mankind killed by fire, smoke and sulfur (second Woe)	Poured on Euphrates River; the water dried up to prepare the way for the kings of the East; Three frog-demons gather the nations for battle against God
7	Silence & Seven Trumpets	Loud voices in heaven; God's temple in heaven opened Judgment (= 3rd Woe)	Poured into the air Lightning, thunder, earthquake

When God rises from his judgment throne to enact the sentence he has pronounced, there will be no complaints, no whining, "That's not fair!" Part of the increase of wickedness in our world is God's way of clarifying the sides. With each passing day, with each vile act which passes seemingly unnoticed, God's judgments are more and more clearly needed. They are more and more clearly defined. And one of these days, when they are finally poured out, there will be none left who says, "But we just didn't have a chance to repent. We just didn't know!"

And now, the event we've all been waiting for . . . the grand entrance of God. He prepares for his coming in the most unusual way. With the sixth seal he dries up the river Euphrates. This too is strangely reminiscent of the Exodus. He ushers in the kings of the East and several demonic frogs to the mountain of Megiddo, that is Armageddon (cf. Ezek 38–39). And the questions begin to flurry. Who are these kings? Where is Armageddon? What do the frogs stand for? Endless discussions try to identify these entities. The bottom line is that our best guesses remain just that — guesses. Suffice to say here that God moves kings and demons like pawns on a chessboard. That, it seems, is the important lesson, not the identification of these evil warriors. It is God, not they, who is center stage in this scene, so let's keep the center stage in focus. Besides, they'll be whisked off to their demise as quickly as they arise.

Here's where it gets good. God leads these wicked warriors to set up battle lines against each other. They hate God and no doubt intend to demolish him. But they wind up destroying their own allies in a civil war of Satanic forces. Thus, much of God's "dirty work" is done by his enemies against his enemies. It's a beautiful thing to watch! God doesn't even lift a finger, except to point and laugh! Once he has them all in one place, God makes his grand entrance. When he does, the thunder rolls, the earth shakes, the cities are shattered, and kings scattered. The mountains flee, and the sky spits

At this point we can either change our view of God or rewrite the pages of Scripture.

out one hundred pound hailstones. God's judgment ensues. One side cheers, the other wails.

Each of the three cycles seems to follow the same pattern. The first five describe what takes place on the earth. The sixth points to one last galactic conflict. The seventh is a picture of God's final judgment. Thus the bowls set the stage for the rest of the book, what we might call "A Tale of Two Cities." *One last question looms large: Do you know which side you are on?*

One last question looms large: Do you know which side you are on?

REFLECTING ON LESSON SEVEN

1. What is the purpose of the seven seals (6–7), the seven trumpets (8–9), and the seven bowls and plagues (15–16)?

2. How do you respond to this idea that God has a temper? Could God be a God of love without being a God of wrath?

3. List all the similarities you can between the Exodus events and Rev. 15–16.

4. Using the chart on p. 67, what are the similarities and differences between the three cycles of sevens?

5. Why will no one be able to whine or complain at the judgment seat of God?

6. In your own words, express what positive benefits arise from the ashes of human suffering and pain. (There may be many correct responses; pull as many as you can from the principles found in Revelation, especially these three cycles of seven.)

7. Do you know which side you're on?

8

EIGHT

THE DESTINY OF THE DAMNED

One of the most frustrating things in times of tribulation is when the wicked prosper. When it looks like evil people get away with stuff, the saints just cringe. Well, in the next four chapters of Revelation, the Dragon, the Beast and the Harlot get what's coming to them.

STRIKE ONE

As chapter 17 opens, we come face to face with a harlot. Boy is she a looker! She has an entourage of kings she's seduced. She rides mounted atop the beast of chapter 13, bedecked with purple garments and draped with gold, pearls and precious stones. Like a good Roman prostitute, she has a title on her forehead. It reads: Mystery, Babylon the Great, the Mother of Prostitutes and of the Abominations of the Earth. In her hand is a cup of filth and she is drunk with the blood of the saints.

Isn't that a pretty picture! What does it mean? *Fortunately,* John explains the meaning of this vision in 17:8-14. *Unfortunately,* his explanation is more cryptic than his portrait. Who are these ten kings? Is that some kind of league of nations? Or does it describe a series of Roman Emperors? What and where are these seven hills? And who is this eighth king?

The Antichrist? A brief survey of the literature on Revelation at this point illustrates the fact that for every Ph.D. there is an equal and opposite Ph.D. There has been much speculation about the ten kings, their seven hills, and especially this eighth king who was, is not, but will rise to destruction.

Obviously, we'll not settle the mysteries of the universe in the next paragraph or two. Nonetheless, we can know with some degree of certainty a couple of things about John's cryptic vision. First, the beast we have here is pretending to be God, the ever-living One, who was and is and is to come (1:4, 8; 4:8). Yet the beast falls far short. Three times he is identified as the one who once was, now is not, and will rise again but only for judgment (17:8, 11). It appears that God is mocking him. Indeed, he did rule, but now is powerless and when he does reappear it will only be for sentencing. Second, this eighth king is the beast on whom the harlot rests. For all practical purposes, this beast is the devil incarnate. That's why it says that he belongs to the other seven kings (17:11). He is their figurehead and hero. He is the real power behind the earthly rulers that carry out his program. Then, right on the heels of these seven kings we have ten more. John may have had ten specific rulers in mind either of his own day or some future era. If he did, however, it is surely lost on most readers of Revelation. More likely we should weigh these rulers rather than count them. After all, both numbers, seven and ten, are highly symbolic. They have to do with completeness. With that in mind, these seventeen kings shake down something like this: *All earthly emperors which rule through Satan's impetus will share in his destruction.*

Back to the issue at hand — the prostitute. Undoubtedly John's Jewish audience would have heard the term "prostitute" and remembered Hosea's words about Israel (also Jer 3:1-3; Ezek 16:15-41, etc.). So some say this wicked woman is a symbol of the corrupt Jewish religious system. The problem is that she also looks an awful lot like Rome. After all, she works in conjunction with the beast and is called Babylon; both codes were connected

All earthly emperors which rule through Satan's impetus will share in his destruction.

72

with Rome in John's day. Likely, then, this madam is a symbol of false religion in general, whether she appears in the form of Jewish orthodoxy gone bad or Roman paganism run amuck. Furthermore, she functions in the same way as the beast from the land in chapter 13.

The pagan culture that surrounds us will not last forever.

She both uses and promotes the beast out of the sea. In other words, like chapter 13 we have false religion and pagan government playing off each other. Earlier the beast of pagan government got the accent. Here, the harlot of false religion takes center stage.

This chapter, however, is not how the two work together, but what punishment will befall them. That's where it really gets interesting. Verse 16 says that the beast will hate the harlot, cannibalize her flesh, and burn her carcass with fire. The saints stand on the sideline and cheer. Our enemy, the prostitute, is destroyed by her own ally. Is that possible? Yes. In fact, if we take a look around, we will see how true these words are. Pagan government will use false religion for its own ends. But when it is through with her, the beast will persecute false religion just as soundly as it does Christianity. The best part is yet to come. Listen: "For God has put it into their hearts to accomplish his purpose by agreeing to give the beast their power to rule, until God's words are fulfilled" (17:17). God divides the enemy's ranks and pits them against each other. They implode on themselves. All we do is stand and watch. God doesn't lift a finger. He merely plants the seed in his enemies' minds and they do the rest.

So much for false religion. Yet the song of destruction continues in chapter 18, with pagan culture, represented by Babylon. These two go hand in hand, you know. That is to say, the prostitute of false religion and pagan culture, under the banner of Babylon, are kissin' cousins. They work in tandem to seduce the saints of God to get marked by the beast.

The kings of the earth (18:9) bemoan the demise of Babylon. So do the merchants (18:11) and every sea captain (18:17). They are losing their commerce in the "finer things of life."

The whole earth laments her demise. But heaven rejoices and calls the saints to join in (18:20-24). *The pagan culture that surrounds us will not last forever.* That's the meaning of chapter 18. But the purpose of this chapter is stated in 18:4: "Come out of her, my people, so that you will not share in her sins, so that you will not receive any of her plagues." Could it be any simpler? Get out of the prostitute's bed, or you'll lie with her in her suffering. This chapter is a serious call to holiness. As God's people we must be set apart. We cannot afford to participate with the world in their program, entertainments, divergences, or business. This is not a call to a monastery, but it is a call to a counter-culture.

STRIKE TWO

The harlot and her city just bit the dust. Now the beast is about to go. Chapter 19 opens with the great "Hallelujah" chorus. In fact, these first six verses contain the only four uses of the word in all the N.T. Heaven is ecstatic because they are about to celebrate the wedding feast of the Lamb. "Let us rejoice and be glad and give him glory! For the wedding of the Lamb has come, and his bride as made herself ready" (19:7).

So when heaven opens up, you expect to see a bridegroom step out, dressed in a tux and ready for a wedding. That's not what we get, however. Out rides a king in full battle array. The beast summons the lords of the earth. Their armies prepare for battle. We expect shields clashing and mortar fire . . . Nothing! To our surprise, *there is no battle of Armageddon, just a slaughter of God's opposition.* This is the most one-sided battle of all human history. The beast and the false prophet are captured and thrown into the lake of fire. The sword from Jesus' mouth slaughters the rest and the birds of the air feast on their flesh. It is gruesome and glorious all at once.

STRIKE THREE

There is no *battle* of Armageddon, just a slaughter of God's opposition.

We're rid of the beast and the harlot. Two down, one to go. It's time to slay the Dragon. Without a doubt chapter 20

74

is the most controversial chapter of Revelation, perhaps of the whole Bible. The story line is really quite simple, however. The devil is bound for a thousand years in the Abyss. After that, he is released for a short time. He wreaks havoc among the nations and gathers Gog and Magog for battle. *Fire from heaven consumes them and all the bad guys are thrown into the lake of fire. THE END.*

Fire from heaven consumes them and all the bad guys are thrown into the lake of fire. THE END.

Two things complicate matters here. First, does chapter 20 follow chapter 19 chronologically? Or do they tell the same story from different angles? Second, do we take the thousand years literally? Or do we look at it as a "long period of time"?

The two dominant views on this chapter go something like this. View #1: After a literal seven year tribulation period, Jesus will come back to earth. Satan will be bound in the Abyss for a thousand years. During that time Jesus will reign on *this* earth as a global dictator in Jerusalem. For a literal millennium there will be world peace, unprecedented prosperity, and a number of supernatural changes in our natural world such as wolves lying down with lambs. At the end of the thousand years, Satan will be released. He will rally his troops for a final battle against Jesus' kingdom. The devil will lose, of course. Then the earth will be destroyed, the judgment will be enacted and both the new Jerusalem and the lake of fire will finally be inhabited.

The second view is radically different. It suggests that these descriptions are figurative. After all, the book of Revelation, like other Apocalyptic literature, is code language which deals with symbols rather than literal descriptions. Thus, the thousand years represents the long period of time in which the church, by the preaching of the gospel, thwarts Satan's work of deception, intimidation, and accusation against the redeemed. This is presently taking place. Satan's work is "bound" by the preaching of the gospel and the growth of God's kingdom on this earth. In particular, Satan is bound from deceiving the nations (20:3 & 8). And, in fact, it appears that the preaching of the gospel is doing just that. Where the Bible flourishes, Satanic deception diminishes. After the "thousand" years are ended (i.e., after the church age), there will be a brief period of "End Time" chaos where God will give Satan more liberty to deceive the nations (cf. 1 Tim 4:1-3). But then Jesus will come back and destroy the devil and his advocates. The earth and its works will be burnt up, judgment carried out and the New Jerusalem and the lake of fire inhabited — all on the same day!

Both views have strong advocates, men and women of intelligence, faith, and devotion. Both views have a bunch of other Bible passages that support their position. And both views have some serious flaws. We may have to await the return of Christ to settle the issue (as if we would care about it then). Our purpose here is not to outline eschatology but to ask, "How does this text function in the body of Christ?" In other words, we are more concerned here with "What should we do about it?" than "What does it mean?"

Perhaps instead of asking, "What do the 'experts' say about this text?" we might get farther asking, "How would this text be read by those in suffering?" *How would a widow in China read this chapter after her husband was martyred for preaching Jesus?* How would a teenage Christian in the Sudan read this passage when faced with the option of losing his family for faith in Christ? How would the evangelical businessman in Latin America read these words when all his customers abandoned him after his conversion? This chapter has three essential messages for each of these believers. When they read about Satan being bound, surely they would say, "He's not today! In fact, he is let loose on me!" In the face of such Satanic attack, these words would, oddly enough, bring comfort.

How would a widow in China read chapter 20 after her husband was martyred for preaching Jesus?

First, while Satan is let loose on me now, it won't last for long. While his binding may have been for a thousand years, his free reign of terror is brief. If I can just hold on to Jesus a little longer, I can outlive Satan's onslaught. Second, though Satan attacks me, he is not in control. God bound him, God released him, and God will destroy him. It is God who holds the controls to time and eternity. It is God who holds my life in his hands. Though my suffering seems unbearable, God is in control, not the devil. If I can just trust him, he will sustain me through such tribulation. Third, God will repay Satan for every evil deed he's ever done. He will face the full fury of God's wrath for sure. One doesn't have to be mean-spirited for ultimate justice to be comforting. Even in a secular courtroom, the crowd often spontaneously applauds when an insufferable criminal is sentenced. If I hold on to Jesus, he will right all these wrongs soon and very soon.

> The torment of hell is too dark for words. The beauty of heaven is more blissful than can be imagined.

Theologically, this chapter is a bear! Pastorally, it is a masterpiece of comfort for those who are suffering. I suppose that when we look at it intellectually from air-conditioned ivory towers, we will inevitably argue over its meaning. But when these words are shoved into the crucible of Christian persecution, they have unmistakable clarity and unparalleled beauty.

THREE STRIKES — YOU'RE OUT!

We may debate the meaning of 20:1-10. However verses 11-15 are crystal clear. There will be a day of judgment. The first book to be opened is a record of our deeds. All people, great and small, will be judged based on what they have done. None will be saved, however, because of their good deeds recorded in the first book. Rather, we will be saved because our names are written in the second book, the book of Life. Through the blood of Jesus our names are recorded. Anyone who refuses to accept his love will find themselves cast into the lake of fire. This business of hell is too serious to ignore. *Its torment is too dark for words.* We had better pay attention to these warnings before it's too late. Conversely, *the beauty of heaven is more blissful than can be imagined.* Wisdom calls for us to choose now to follow God. Our temporary passage on this earth is so brief in the shadow of the life to come. Should we have to suffer for Christ, it will be as nothing compared to the extremes of eternity.

REFLECTING ON LESSON EIGHT

1. What two things can we know with relative certainty about the beast and the eighth king?

2. Who is the prostitute? What does she do? How is she destroyed?

3. What does Babylon represent? What happens when she falls?

4. How does the picture of Jesus in Chapter 19 differ from his earthly ministry?

5. What two things complicate our interpretation of Revelation 20? Summarize the two dominant views of this passage.

6. How does this text actually function in the lives of those who are suffering? What does it cause them to do? What are the three messages of comfort from this chapter?

7. Paraphrase the description of judgment given in Rev 20:11-15. Compare this to Matt 25:31-46. What role do our good deeds play in our judgment?

9
N I N E

COMING ATTRACTIONS

When Jesus comes back, we're not going to heaven. Read Revelation 21:1-3, "Then I saw a new heaven and a new earth, for the first heaven and the first earth had passed away. And there was no longer any sea. I saw the Holy City, the new Jerusalem, coming down out of heaven from God, prepared as a bride beautifully dressed for her husband. And I heard a loud voice from the throne saying 'Now the dwelling of God is with men, and he will live with them.'"

It is true that much of Revelation is highly figurative. Yet these figures describe realities. In other words, some of these descriptions of the New Jerusalem may simply be the best John can come up with given our earthly understanding and limited vocabulary (e.g., streets of gold). Nevertheless, the reality behind these descriptions is very real.

So what does this mean? It means that when Jesus returns, we are not going to go to heaven but to the New Jerusalem which will be established on the new earth. That is a wonderful thought. If we were to go to heaven, especially as it is typically pictured, wouldn't it get rather boring? After all, we would all be dressed in white sitting on cloud nine. (Why cloud nine? I can see why not cloud 666. But cloud seven would seem more appropriate). And what do we do up there for all eternity? We sing. Listen, after some of the song services I've endured I'm convinced that eternal congregational singing may, in fact, be the other place!

So there we sit, singing. We go through every song in the song book . . . twice. We even have time to sing all those third verses that we never sang down here. So that takes about three days. What do we do then? We sing it again! After a year or so we get bored. So we start picking up those denominational hymn books. Why, we even submit to singing choruses. After awhile we'll have to sing the German songs and Latin Gregorian chants. Yet even they will eventually be exhausted. But you know what the song says, "When we've been there ten thousand years, bright shining as the sun, we've no less days to sing God's praise than when we've first begun!" Oh great!

Please don't misunderstand, *the praise of God will be immensely satisfying. To worship him for all eternity will never become boring.* But to reduce worship to singing alone is both boring and unbiblical. The portrait of the New Jerusalem here in chapters 21-22 tells of a city on a physical earth. That makes a lot of sense since the word of God promises us resurrected bodies (1 Cor 15). Imagine it, Eden will be restored. There will be agriculture and architecture, culture and art, plants, animals, camping, rivers, homes and entertainment. Can you imagine what a wonderful place this world would be without sin? That's what the New Earth will be like. Can you imagine how technologically advanced we would be if we weren't distracted with war, medicine, police protection, and government. We may well have technological advancements in the New Jerusalem that far exceed what we have or even imagine here. God is not opposed to our curiosity or creativity; he gave them both to us. As Solomon said, "It is the glory of God to conceal a matter; to search out a matter is the glory of kings" (Prov 25:2). Just think of it, an eternal game of hide and go seek, show and tell, and follow the leader.

> The praise of God will be immensely satisfying. To worship him for all eternity will never become boring.

Up to this point, I've simply suggested that the New Jerusalem is a real, tangible world and that our bodies will also be real (though spiritual and transformed), whatever that looks like. One day I was out calling with one of my elders, a former physicist for NASA. The subject of this city came up and I said, "John, can you imagine the elevator system in a city that is 1,400 miles square." He asked, "Doesn't the Bible say that our bodies will be like Christ's resurrected body?" "Well, yes" I said (Phil 3:21). Then he asked, "So why do you think we will need elevators?" Obviously the nature of our new bodies is speculative, but suddenly the possibilities become **very** interesting.

> While there will be astounding diversity, there will be no racism or parochialism.

So what will the new Jerusalem be like? Revelation describes it in terms of what *isn't* there and in terms of what *is* there.

WHAT ISN'T THERE

In the New Jerusalem there will be no unemployment, picket lines, police, politicians, doctors, lawyers (no kidding!), preachers (praise God), prisons, hospitals, IRS, INS, CIA, FBI, Rustoleum, mothballs, locks, Kleenex, light bulbs, weddings, funerals, or armies . . . just to name a few. These last two chapters get even more specific.

(1) There will no longer be any sea (21:1). Earlier the "many waters" were used to describe many peoples, tongues and languages. That seems reasonable. In the ancient world, seas were dangerous places that kept people apart. They hindered the wealth of commerce and the wonders of other cultures. In the New Earth there will be no separation of peoples. *While there will be astounding diversity, there will be no racism or parochialism.* From where I stand, that looks pretty good.

(2) There will be no tears nor death, no crying nor pain (21:4). No cancer allowed. No funerals, divorces, murders, thefts, gossip, broken dreams, unresolved anger, haunting memories, or lifelong regrets from momentary sins.

81

(3) There is no more going to church (21:22). We will dwell eternally in God's presence. We won't have to chase after him through priests or liturgies. No more "daily devotions" or sermon outlines. All of those shadows will be consumed in his glorious reality.

(4) There is no more sun or moon (21:23). God himself will provide all the light we need.

(5) Nothing impure will enter the New Jerusalem (21:27). So how can we expect to get in? Obviously, the blood of Jesus purifies us. What a majestic thought! However, it may be even more magnificent than *"mere"* sanctification. Is it possible that we could be sinless in our new bodies? Is it possible that Jesus will no longer have to serve as my advocate with the Father? That sounds more like a fairytale than eternal life! Nevertheless, those things which cause me to sin will no longer exist. First of all, Satan and his cronies don't get a guest pass. They will no longer put ideas in my mind and opportunities in my path. Granted, I'm perfectly capable of sinning all by myself. But God's enemies help me out exponentially. Without them, I'll be a lot closer to perfection. Second, I won't live in a society where sin prevails. There will be no more lewd billboards or aggressive drivers with fingers flying out their windows. There are no red-light districts or adult book stores, no materialistic malls or Hollywood to promote self-aggrandizement and the exploitation of sensual lusts. Because my environment will be purified and my mind transformed, I will come pretty close to perfection. Third, there will be no marriage or giving in marriage. The Bible does not say that we will be asexual in heaven. But the nature of our sexuality will be transformed. Sexuality is a God-given gift and it is good. Yet who could deny that it is one of the primary means by which Satan leads people astray? Without my present passions I will come a lot closer to sinlessness. Fourth, there will be no competition in heaven. I am at my very best when I truly worship God. It doesn't happen nearly often enough. But every once in a while I am acutely aware of God's

The New Jerusalem will lack everything that hinders us from full righteousness.

presence. It is then that I have my best thoughts, then that I am the most humble yet the most like Jesus. Because we will dwell perpetually in the presence of God, our thoughts will be higher, our motives nobler, our spirits humbler. We can be sinless. There is one last thing. It is time. Often we prioritize projects rather than people. We listen poorly and work haphazardly because we are pressed by a clock. In eternity, what's the rush? We will always have time to listen to a child's story, to hold a loved one's hand, to sit quietly and watch the world. There will be no deadlines to meet, no traffic jams to beat, no lines to rush to the front of. It sounds too good to be true. Nevertheless, *the New Jerusalem will lack everything that hinders us from full righteousness.*

God will put an end to the inequality between the sexes.

(6) There will be no curse (22:3). For both men and women this means there is no more death. For men it also means that we won't earn a living by the sweat of our brow. For women, there will be no more pain in childbirth. But there is something else. God told Eve that she would "desire" her husband but that he would rule over her. We read the word "desire" and hear good things. We picture a woman in an evening gown with a candlelight dinner waiting for her man when he comes home. Wrong! This particular word translated "desire" is only used twice in the O.T. It is found in the curse passage just referenced (Gen 3:16). Then in the very next chapter (4:7), God says to Cain, "[S]in is crouching at the door; it *desires* to have you." So we picture a woman crouched behind the door with curlers, barbed wire and a rolling pin, desiring to bludgeon the sucker as he walks through the door. This tension between the sexes is part of the curse. Praise God that it is alleviated in Jesus Christ (cf. Gal 3:28). It is alleviated, but not eradicated. There are still differences in men's and women's roles in the church. Furthermore, Christian women still struggle with this desire to dominate and sadly, still lose in a big way. It is still primarily women who get lower paying jobs, who get raped, who are beaten by husbands, who are saddled with domestic

responsibilities which they often bear alone. They just can't win — they are under a curse. In heaven, however, all this will change. There will be no more competition, fighting, or suffering. *God will put an end to the inequality between the sexes.*

WHAT WILL BE THERE

Heaven will be a wonderful place for all that isn't there. But *our hearts yearn for heaven because of what is there.* There will be saints of old in heaven: Abraham, Isaac, Jacob; Peter, James, and John. Oh, the conversations we will have! Moreover, there are many loved ones there. Wives will be reunited with husbands. Granted, the nature of their relationship will change, but how sweet it will be. Fathers will see children who died in their cribs. Grandparents will introduce themselves to grandchildren who only knew them through pictures and stories. As sweet as this reunion will be, however, that's not why we want to go there.

There will be wealth that is unimaginable. John describes the city of vast proportions with boggling wealth (21:18-21). Even the asphalt is twenty-four karat gold! The angelic choirs will be . . . well, heavenly! The new earth will surely put this one to shame (and God didn't do half bad on this one!). None will lack for food. Everyone is a prince and princess in the kingdom of God. We all dream of such luxury and comfort. However, that's not why we want to go there.

We will have new bodies. No more arthritis, no more physical limitations, no more looking in the mirror and asking "Why?" We will have energy to work and play, time to rest and worship. As wonderful as this sounds, this is not why we want to go there.

We want to go there because *he* is there. He is there. This one we have talked about, sung to, read of, written for. He is waiting with outstretched arms and these words: "Well done, good and faithful servant. Enter into the joy of your reward." Yet I can't help but think that one glimpse of his person will make all of our words irrelevant. He is so much grander than we

Our hearts yearn for heaven because of what *is* there.

84

have described, much more glorious than we have imagined. Our impulse will not be to embrace him as a buddy, but to fall down at his feet awed, fearful, convulsing in the majesty of the moment. I suspect that it will only be his immense love that draws us to our feet to receive his embrace.

Here, then, is the most amazing truth of all eternity: God loves you.

Heaven is better than you think, and it is sooner than you think. Jesus says, "Behold, I am coming soon!" (22:7). "The time is near" (22:10). "Behold, I am coming soon!" (22:12). "Yes, I am coming soon" (22:20). His impassioned plea is that we come to him. "The Spirit and the Bride say 'Come!' And let him who hears say, 'Come!' Whoever is thirsty, let him come; and whoever wishes, let him take the free gift of the water of life."

Here, then, is the most amazing truth of all eternity: God loves you. In fact, he doesn't just love you, he really, really likes you. He invites you to him because he craves your presence (21:3). So what can we say in reply to the God of the universe who invites us to come? What can we say but, "Come, Lord Jesus" (22:20)?

REFLECTING ON LESSON NINE

1. How does this idea of a physical earth as our eternal destiny strike you? What kind of work and play would you want to involve yourself in?

2. From 1 Cor 15:35-53; Phil 3:21 and Rev 21:4, what might our new bodies be like?

3. What kind of things will *not* be in heaven? Which three will you be most happy to see eradicated?

4. How is it possible that we may actually be sinless in heaven?

5. What "curses" will be lifted in heaven?

6. List the "sweet" things that will be in heaven. What is the sweeetest of them all?

7. How does it make you feel that God desperately yearns for your presence in heaven?

About the Author

Mark E. Moore earned his Bachelor of Theology degree from Ozark Christian College in 1986 and his Masters in Education from Incarnate Word College in San Antonio, Texas, in 1990. He was the preaching minister of a bilingual congregation in San Antonio from 1986–90. In 1990, he returned to Ozark to open The Learning Center and to teach the Life of Christ, the book of Acts and Bible Interpretation. He is the author of College Press's two-volume set, *The Chronological Life of Christ*. His wife Barbara and two children, Joshua and Megan, are a source of pride and inspiration to him.